TABLE OF CONTENTS

ACRONYMS

CAO	Civil Affairs Operations
CMO	Civil Military Operations
CMOC	Civil Military Operations Center
COA	Course of Action
CR	Civil Reconnaissance
DART	Disaster Assistance Response Team
DC	Dislocated Civilians
FHA	Foreign Humanitarian Assistance
FM	Field Manual
HACC	Humanitarian Assistance Coordination Center
HCA	Humanitarian Civic Action
IDPs	Internally Displaced Civilians
JIIM	Joint, Interagency, Intergovernmental, Multinational
JP	Joint Publication
KWP	Korean Worker's Party
NA	Nation Assistance
OCHA	Office of the Coordinator for Humanitarian Assistance
OFDA	Office of Foreign Disaster Assistance
PDRK	People's Democratic Republic of Korea (North Korea)
PRC	Populace and Resource Control
RoK	Republic of Korea (South Korea)
SCA	Support to Civil Administration
SOCOM	Special Operations Command

SOF   Special Operations Forces

USAID   United States Agency for International Development

ILLUSTRATIONS

Page

TABLES

CHAPTER 1

INTRODUCTION

North Korea is a nightmare state, worse than George Orwell's
1984. . . . If the North Korean state ever completely failed, South Korea
(and by extension the U.S. which has scores of thousands of troops there)
would wake up to a spreading humanitarian crisis, with millions streaming
over the demilitarized zone seeking food and shelter.

— Michael Dougherty

Background

Creation of Two Koreas

After the United States and Union of Soviet Socialist Republics forces defeated

the Japanese during World War II, the two countries determined who controlled which

part of the Korean peninsula at the 38th Parallel. The Soviets controlled the North and the

United States controlled the South.[1] The United Nations intended to hold a democratic

vote by all the Korean people on the type of government it would have as an independent

country in 1948. At the behest of Kim Il Sung, Joseph Stalin and the Soviet Union vetoed

the United Nations resolution, and Korea remained split on the 38th parallel.[2] The area

controlled by the Soviets north of the 38th parallel officially became the Democratic

People's Republic of Korea.

The same year, The Korean Worker's Party (KWP) supported a communist coup

in the Republic of Korea. The coup attempt by communists failed and Sigmun Rhee's

government remained in control of South Korea.[3] Kim Il Sung founded the Korean

Worker's Party in 1949 and the KWP quickly established power in the Democratic

People's Republic of Korea (DPRK). That same year, Kim Il Sung nationalized North

1

Korean industry and began purges to secure his hold on the country. By the end of 1949, Kim Il Sung nationalized 90 percent of North Korean industry.[4]

Additionally, Kim began purging the "capitalist collaborators." According to Oh and Hassig, "Even members of Kim's own guerilla band who had fought alongside him in China during the Japanese occupation were purged, leaving Kim the undisputed master of his country."[5] Most of the collaborators were business owners, South Koreans who had fled North after the failed coup attempt, and North Korean leaders who fought with the Chinese and not Kim during World War II.[6]

The United States removed the preponderance of its forces from the Republic of Korea by the end of 1949 putting the onus on the Republic of Korea for its own defense.[7] Kim Il Sung approached Stalin about invading South Korea and Mao promised to provide resources to North Korea. By 25 June 1950, the North Korean Army began its offensive against South Korea. After several months of fighting, United Nations forces led by the United States pushed North Korean forces against the Yalu River triggering an attack by China. After the fighting pushed back and forth across the 38th parallel resulting in a stalemate, the United Nations, the Republic of Korea, the People's Democratic Republic of Korea and China signed an armistice on 27 July 1953.[8] In the eyes of Kim Il Sung, the war was justified as his intent was to liberate Koreans in the south from an oppressive foreign dominated government. Kim called the war the "Fatherland Liberation War."[9]

Following the war, Kim Il Sung again focused on consolidating power in DPRK. One of the methods key to securing power for him in North Korea was the development of Juche, or Self Reliance. Kim Il Sung focused national resources on the development of the military industrial base. The building of military capability was part of Kim's defense first policy. He did this to gain independence from China and the Soviet Union by ending North Korea's dependency on the two countries for military resources. Kim Il Sung was a charismatic leader who dubbed himself the "Great Leader." In 1980, Kim Il Sung

announced that Kim Jong Il was going to be his successor and was the "Dear Leader" and

wove the familial succession as part of Juche. The North Korean Party's explanation for

the selection of Kim Jong Il was that Kim Jong Il was the most acquainted with Kim Il

Sung's Juche philosophy and was also the eldest son.[10]

Kim Il Sung combined political ideology with Confucian philosophy to guarantee

that the Kim Family would control the Workers Party of Korea.[11] The North Korean

Press often refers to the combination of the two ideologies as the "Kim Il Sung Nation."[12]

Kim Il Sung was named President for eternity, and the office of President became mostly

ceremonial following the death of Kim Il Sung in 1994. Kim Jong Il maintained power

through the control of the Workers Party of Korea.[13]

The Economic and Development Divide

The development of collectivist farming and focusing all of North Korea's

industrial economy on building military capability rapidly impoverished the country.

Article 23 of the PDRK constitution called for the state seizing all private land for the

people.[14] Article 34 dictated priorities for industrial production starting military

equipment and ending with consumer use items.[15] In 1998, Kim Jong Il announced he

was going to continue the military first policy despite severe food shortages.[16] By the

1990s, North Korea was almost completely dependent on foreign food aid. Prior to 1995,

North Koreans would eat fish or meat two to three times a year and usually only on Kim

Il Sung or Kim Jong Il's birthdays. Following 1995, the state stopped issuing meals with

meat or fish.[17] Malnutrition and starvation in North Korea is so rampant that the average

North Korean is six inches shorter than their South Korean counterparts. Humanitarian organizations believe that the development of the North Korean people has been stunted for several generations.[18]

Due to economic stagnation and food shortage issues, many experts continue to speculate about the possibility of a collapse in North Korea despite its apparent resilience. In a *New York Times* article, Choe Sang-Hun points to widespread unrest leading to open protests in Pyongyang.[19] The speculation of a North Korean collapse has only increased in the new millennium since the rapid increase of North Korean defections, from a few hundred a year in the nineties to a couple of thousand a year after 2002,[20] and events like the 2009 riots after North Korea reevaluated its currency.[21] Adding to that speculation is the short amount of time Kim Jong Un has been able to consolidate power before his father Kim Jong Il passed away. Kim Jong Il was a member of the Korea Workers Party for 24 years and the official heir to Kim Il Sung for 13 years before his father's death. Kim Jong Il was also the eldest son which fits with Confucian tradition.[22]

Kim Jong Un has neither of those advantages. Kim Jong Un was a member of the KWP for four years and a four star general for 15 months before Kim Jong Il's death. Additionally, Kim Jong Il is the third son. Kim Jong Il does not have the additional advantage of Confucian tradition.[23] Seung-Ho Joo, editor of Inha University's *Journal of International Studies* contends, "Internal problems, such as poverty, corruption, bureaucratic inertia, and power struggle, will prove lethal to the regime."

North Korea's control mechanisms are weakening, the country is suffering a food shortage, and the country is transitioning to a young ruler. All of those issues contribute to a future collapse. The possibility of a collapse in the near term increases the importance of planning for a post collapse response. This study will determine what role

United States civil affairs (CA) may play in a greater United States response in support of its South Korean ally.

Theories of a Collapse

Despite the apparent resilience of the North Korean Regime, most experts still agree that there will be an eventual collapse. The Strategic Studies Institute commissioned Dr. Andrew Scobell, an international relations professor at Texas A&M University, to write a monograph on possible scenarios of a possible North Korean Collapse. Dr. Andrew Scobell states that while regimes are often resilient, they are also brittle and burn out is inevitable. Dr Scobell went on to say, "Pyongyang is best described as a failing or eroding totalitarian regime where exhaustion, loosening of central control, and weakening of the monopoly of information are taking their toll."[24]

Two aspects to the collapse are worth understanding in context; however this paper will not speculate on when or what type of collapse will occur. Dr. Scobell describes the collapse of a totalitarian regime as a process and not an outcome.[25] Dr. Scobell uses the term "landing" to frame the impacts at the end of the collapse process. The hard landing stipulates that North Korea continues with all of its previous policies with no reforms and that the country is not prepared for a post collapse transition. This form of landing will take everyone in Pyongyang and those who watch it by surprise.[26] The soft landing acknowledges that North Korea could make greater reforms than the special economic zones on the Chinese border that would also encompass the entire country. These reforms would lessen the hardship and possibly open North Korea to the outside world. Some experts believe that a soft landing could make the post collapse much easier from an economic, psychological and humanitarian standpoint.[27]

The type of landing is less important to this study than the outcomes after the landing. Either scenario could lead to some form of war. Seeing its demise coming, DPRK could attack South Korea to allow the elites to negotiate surrender on favorable terms. An impending power struggle among the elites could lead to a civil war.[28] Either version of a collapse will leave a humanitarian crisis that will require international intervention.

Importance of the Study

United States planners need to conduct more detailed planning for the humanitarian issues the Republic of Korea and its allies will face following the regime's collapse. The United States military was unprepared to assist in a recent humanitarian response of large magnitude and should learn from the lessons learned to prepare for future crisis. In 2010, relief organizations were not prepared to deal with the nearly 1.3 million IDPs in Haiti and three years later most of the still remain homeless.[29] IDPs could potentially number as high as five million following a collapse of the North Korean Regime.[30] The sheer number of displaced people alone could be overwhelming without considering food, water, and other essential services. The subject is of immense importance to the United States because of the likely monetary and human costs of responding to a humanitarian crisis. It is essential planners carefully consider the role of a limited resource like civil affairs (CA) in a response to the collapse. This paper will show a niche role for United States civil affairs forces in the impending humanitarian disaster following the collapse of the North Korean Regime.

Assumptions

A few assumptions frame the topic and allow analysis of a United States civil affairs effort assisting with a post collapse North Korea and Korean Unification.

The first assumption is that The Republic of Korea will request United States assistance early as a Regime collapse seems to be eminent. The Republic of Korea is a sovereign country, and the United States cannot send any additional forces without a request for additional forces. The United States and the Republic of Korea already have treaties and military plans in place to facilitate the request for forces.[31] An early request for additional United States military assistance will give the United States the time to preposition conventional forces and humanitarian assets in South Korea.

The second assumption is that the security environment after the collapse will be semi-permissive. The humanitarian response will happen after any conventional combat if there is an explosive collapse. The threat level will be non-permissive for any civilian aid agencies to operate during any combat operations after the collapse of the regime. There is a possibility hard line members of the North Korean military will conduct irregular warfare following the collapse, but the threat is not likely to be persistent.[32] The possibility of an irregular threat will not likely deter civilian aid organizations from providing assistance, but may limit their scope or the distance from secured areas they are willing to work. This paper will not attempt to conduct a thorough analysis of the security environment. Assuming a semi-permissive security environment is important to assessing the nature of a humanitarian response following a collapse of the North Korean Regime and the different capabilities United States military organizations bring to a humanitarian response.

Definition of Terms

CAO. civil affairs operations as those military operations conducted by civil affairs forces that (1) enhance the relationship between military forces and civil authorities in localities where military forces are present; (2) require coordination with other interagency organizations, intergovernmental organizations, nongovernmental organizations, indigenous populations and institutions, and the private sector; and (3) involve application of functional specialty skills that normally are the responsibility of civil government to enhance the conduct of civil-military operations.

CMO. Defines civil-military operations as the activities of a commander that establish, maintain, influence, or exploit relations between military forces, governmental and nongovernmental civilian organizations and authorities, and the civilian populace in a friendly, neutral, or hostile operational area in order to facilitate military operations, to consolidate and achieve operational U.S. objectives. Civil-military operations may include performance by military forces of activities and functions normally the responsibility of the local, regional, or national government.[33]

CR. Civil Reconnaissance is a targeted, planned, and coordinated observation and evaluation of specific civil aspects of the environment. CR focuses on the civil component, the elements of which are best represented by the acronym ASCOPE: area, structures, capabilities, organizations, people, and events. Priority information requirements focus on CR for the purpose of collecting civil information to enhance situational understanding and facilitate decision-making.[34]

DMZ. The Demilitarized Zone in Korea runs along the 38th parallel starting at the mouth of the Imjin River. The DMZ is the most heavily mined border in the world. The

United States has a designated Joint Security Area at Panmunjom where talks between North and South Korea occur.[35]

FHA. Foreign Humanitarian Assistance are programs conducted to relieve or reduce the results of natural or man-made disasters or other endemic conditions, such as human pain, disease, hunger, or need that might present a serious threat to life or that can result in great damage to or loss of property. Normally, FHA includes humanitarian services and transportation; the provision of food, clothing, medicine, beds and bedding; temporary shelter and housing; the furnishing of medical materiel and medical and technical personnel; and making repairs to essential services.[36]

IDP. Internally displaced persons are "persons or groups of persons who have been forced or obliged to flee or to leave their homes or places of habitual residence, in particular as a result of or in order to avoid the effects of armed conflict, situations of generalized violence, violations of human rights or natural or human-made disasters, and who have not crossed an internationally recognized State border."[37]

Juche. In Korean, the term means "self-reliance." The three aspects of Juche are philosophical independence, economic independence, and strong national defense. The inception of the ideology places Kim Il Sung, the Great Leader, and Kim Jong Il, the Dear Leader, as deity like figures in the North Korean mythos.[38]

NA. Nation Assistance is civil or military assistance (other than FHA) rendered to a nation by U.S. forces within that nation's territory during peacetime, crises or emergencies, or war based on agreements mutually concluded between the United States and that nation. NA operations support a HN by promoting sustainable development and growth of responsive institutions. The goal is to promote long-term regional stability.[39]

10

Populace Control. Provides security for the populace, mobilizes human resources, denies enemy access to the population, and detects and reduces the effectiveness of enemy agents. DC operations and NEO are two special categories of populace control that require extensive planning and coordination among various military and nonmilitary organizations.[40]

SCA. Support to Civil Administration are military operations that help to stabilize or to continue the operations of the governing body or civil structure of a foreign country, whether by assisting an established government or by establishing military authority over an occupied population.[41]

Semi-permissive environment. Operational environment in which host government forces, whether opposed or receptive to operations that a unit intends to conduct, do not have totally effective control of the territory and population in the intended operational area.[42]

Thesis Overview

The primary research question asks if there a niche role for United States civil affairs forces in the humanitarian response following the collapse of the North Korean Regime. In order to answer the primary research question, one must first define the true scope of the problem. What is the scope of the humanitarian problem facing South Korea and its allies following the collapse of the North Korean Regime? The economic, infrastructure, and social differences between North and South Korea are stark. Will South Korea's military and civilian aid agencies be able to handle the humanitarian crisis without outside help? Many estimates identify differences between the North and South Korean economies, access to food, and effective health care. Estimates of North Korea's

11

Gross Domestic Product range from 6 percent to 12 percent of South Korea's GDP.[43]

Additionally, it is expected that the total cost of reunification could run from $390 billion (1994 estimate) and $3.2 trillion (1997 estimate) over a ten year-period.[44] The large disparity between the two estimates stems from the uncertainty in the size and volume of the North Korean economy stemming from the closed and secretive nature of the North Korean Government. Additionally, we must consider what issues the disparities between sustenance and infrastructure will have on a humanitarian response. How will commerce be impacted by economic and sustenance issues in North Korea? What is the expected number of migrants to move south for economic opportunities? South Korea and its allies will have to plan for and manage a mass migration south to facilitate a humanitarian response following the collapse. This research will strive to determine the effects that economic poverty, poor agrarian productivity and substandard infrastructure have had on the North Korean population and how those considerations should be integrated into United States planning.

To answer the next secondary question, "What United States doctrine relates to humanitarian issues?," this paper will survey United States military doctrine that relates to a humanitarian response. What United States doctrine either directs civil affairs or indicates a CA capability that would facilitate a response to a humanitarian crisis? Anything the military does should have a foundation in its stated doctrine. Examples of civil affairs core tasks that directly lead to United States civil affairs involvement in humanitarian missions are Foreign Humanitarian Assistance, Populace Control, Civil Information Management, Nation Assistance, and Support to Civil Administration. The Army references CA tasks in FM 3-57 Civil Affairs Operations.[45] Joint doctrine includes

CA Tasks in JP 3-05.[46] USJFK Special Warfare School is the proponent for Army civil affairs Doctrine and Special Operations Command (SOCOM) is the proponent for joint civil affairs doctrine.

Once established what joint and service doctrine says civil affairs should or could do in a humanitarian crisis, additional research will determine what additional capabilities United States civil affairs possess that could be employed to assist following the collapse of the North Korean Regime.

The last portion of research is to determine how United States civil affairs forces have historically been used in a large-scale crisis response capacity. A recent example of a large-scale humanitarian crisis where civil affairs played a significant role was the Haiti earthquake in 2010. The paper will look at the case study to analyze the use of civil affairs in responding to large-scale humanitarian crisis. Even though the anticipated collapse will not be a natural disaster, United States civil affairs forces will encounter many of the same challenges during the response.

Limitations and Delimitations

One of the limitations confronted in researching this paper is classification. All of the research and the resulting analysis in this paper will be unclassified. This paper will not consider any current planning efforts occurring at United States Forces Korea or United States Pacific Command to ensure this paper remains unclassified.

Several delimitations frame this research. The research and analysis will only focus on the use of United States civil affairs. This paper will not consider the role the whole United States military could offer to assist in the impending humanitarian disaster. The scope of the entire United States military involvement is greater than a single paper.

13

Additionally, this research will not consider multinational forces or any other except as it will affect the role of United States civil affairs. The paper will not consider the role of the United States interagency or NGOs unless the organization affects the role United States civil affairs will play after the collapse of the North Korean Regime. This paper will not attempt to speculate on the type of collapse or fall the North Korean Regime will experience. Either scenario will still have a large-scale humanitarian situation to contend with after the collapse. Finally, his paper will not attempt to explain or predict the behavior of international actors and will only mention the roles other countries or organizations may play as it pertains to United States civil affairs operations.

---

[1] Andrea Matles Savada, *North Korea: A Country Study* (Washington, DC: Library of Congress, 1999), 26.

[2] Ibid., 26.

[3] Dan Oh and Ralph C Hassig, *North Korea Through the Looking Glass.* (Washington DC: Brookings Institution Press, 2000), 7.

[4] Savada, *North Korea: A Country Study*, 34.

[5] Oh and Hassig, *North Korea Through the Looking Glass,* 8.

[6] Savada, *North Korea: A Country Study*, 28.

[7] Ibid., 33.

[8] Ibid., 37.

[9] Oh and Hassig, *North Korea Through the Looking Glass,* 9.

[10] Ibid., 10.

[11] Savada, *North Korea: A Country Study*, 41.

[12] Oh and Hassig, *North Korea Through the Looking Glass,* 10.

[13] Savada, *North Korea: A Country Study*, 44.

[14]Oh and Hassig, *North Korea Through the Looking Glass,* 45.

[15]Ibid., 46.

[16]Ibid., 58.

[17]Ibid., 56.

[18]Ibid., 69.

[19]Choe Sang-Hun, "Economic Measures by North Korea Prompt New Hardships and Unrest," *The New York Times*, 4 February 2010.

[20]Tara O, "The Integration of North Korean Defectors in South Korea: Problems and Prospects," *International Journal of Korean Studies*, 155.

[21]Oh and Hassig, *North Korea Through the Looking Glass,* 124.

[22]Savada, *North Korea: A Country Study*, 41.

[23]Seung-Ho Joo, "North Korea under Kim Jong-un: The Beginning of the End of a Peculiar Dynasty," *Pacific Focus*, no. 1 (April 2012): 1.

[24]Scobell, *Projecting Pyang Yang: The Future of North Korea's Kim Jong Il Regime*, x.

[25]Ibid., 25.

[26]Ibid., 26.

[27]Ibid., 19.

[28]Ibid., 28.

[29]Mark Schuller, "Haiti's Disaster after the Disaster: The IDP Camps and Cholera," *The Journal of Humanitarian Assistance* (December 2011), 1.

[30]Seung Mo Choi, *Economic Impacts of Reunifications in Germany and Korea*, Washington State School of Economics, December 2011.

[31]Paul B. Stares and Joel S. Wit, "Preparing for Sudden Change in North Korea," *Council on Foreign Relations* Special Report No. 42 (January 2009), 22.

[32]David S. Maxwell, *Irregular Warfare on the Korean Peninsula: Thoughts on Irregular Threats for North Korea Post-Conflict and Post-Collapse: Understanding*

Them to Counter Them November 2010, http://smallwarsjournal.com/jrnl/art/irregular-warfare-on-the-korean-peninsula (accessed 13 October 2011), 4.

[33]United States Department of the Army, FM 3-57, *Civil Affairs Operations* (Fort Bragg: Department of the Army, 2011), 1-2.

[34]Ibid, 3-11.

[35]Savada, *North Korea: A Country Study*, 74.

[36]United States Department of the Army, FM 3-57, *Civil Affairs Operations*, 3-6.

[37]Walter Kälin, "Guiding Priciples on Internal Displacement," *Studies in Transnational Legal Policy*, no 38 (2008), 2.

[38]Grace Lee, "The Political Philosophy of Juche," *Stanford Journal of East Asian Affiars* 3, no. 1 (2007): 10.

[39]United States Department of the Army, FM 3-57, *Civil Affairs Operations*, 3-13.

[40]Ibid., 3-2.

[41]Ibid., 3-17.

[42]United States Department of the Army, FM 1-02, *Operational Terms and Graphis* (Washington DC: Department of the Army, 2011), 1-138.

[43]Charles Wolf Jr and Kamil Akramov, *North Korean Paradoxes:Circumstances, Costs, and Consequences of Korean Unification* (Santa Monica, CA: RAND, 2005), 16.

[44]Wolf and Akramov, *North Korean Paradoxes:Circumstances, Costs, and Consequences of Korean Unification,* 20.

[45]United States Department of the Army, FM 3-57, *Civil Affairs Operations*, 3-13.

[46]Chairman of the Joint Chiefs of Staff, JP 3-05, *Special Operations,* II-19.

CHAPTER 2

REVIEW OF LITERATURE

Analysis of Literature

This chapter is divided into several subsections to facilitate a discussion of the relevant literature. The first section covers literature that gives background and context to the study on the development of North Korea as a state and why a collapse is likely if not imminent. The second section examines literature that helps describe the scope of the disaster South Korea, the United States, and its allies will likely face after the collapse of North Korea. The third section of this chapter focuses on United States Joint and service Doctrine that will help determine what role United States Forces and United States civil affairs in particular doctrinally play during a humanitarian crisis. The fourth section discusses literature about the Haiti earthquake in 2010. The 2010 Haiti earthquake was a large-scale humanitarian crisis with the collapse of a government that used a significant CA force as part of the United States military response. The final section considers current gaps in the record on humanitarian responses following a collapse of the North Korean regime.

Background

Two books helped frame the historical and socio-political issues that led to the development of the current PDRK and how that helps drive long standing internal and external issues. The first book is *North Korea: A Country Study* by Andrea Matles Savada. The study gives historical context to the development of North Korea's society, government and politics, economy, and national security. The other book essential to developing an understanding of the background of North Korea is a book published by the Brookings Institution, *North Korea Through the Looking Glass*, by Dan Oh and Ralph Hassig. *Through the Looking Glass* provides less historical detail, but a deeper analysis of North Korean ideological, political, and economic development. While the country study was good for getting the basic facts and helping the reader gain an initial understanding of North Korea, Oh and Hassig give the depth and analysis to frame the geopolitical context of North Korea's regime and economy. Having established the context, the next set of literature helps define the scope of the problem following the anticipated collapse.

<u>Scope of the Humanitarian Crisis</u>

A significant amount of literature applies to the first research question on what is the scope of the problem confronting United States civil affairs forces following a collapse of the North Korean Regime. One of the key pieces of literature is a Rand study funded by the United States Department of Defense to build models to determine the costs of Korean Unification. The paper was written by Charles Wolf Jr and Kamil Akramov. The reference that assists scoping the nature of the North Korean problem is a book published by the Brookings Institution, *North Korea Through the Looking Glass*, by Dan Oh and Ralph Hassig.

An economic study, "Economic Impacts of Reunification in Germany and Korea," helps breakdown comparative costs in currency exchanges, currency flight, and the movement of human capital. Of the most significance are the economic models it uses to give several ranges of expected migration from North Korea to South Korea. The paper suggests what it believes will be the most likely percentage of the population to migrate so the number could fluctuate based on the population at the time of the collapse. Additionally, the study describes the infrastructure and services reconstruction that North Korea will require after a collapse. The focus of the study is for economic impacts, but the raw data of development that North Korea will need is pertinent to this study. Seung Mo Choi published the paper at the Washington School of Economics. Stares and Wit published, "Preparing for Sudden Change in North Korea" which is useful in determining the amount of migrants to expect as well as analysis on whether they are likely to migrate to South Korea or China.

The Lancet provided several articles on the health issues facing North Korea. The journal is a resource for the efforts of NGOs across the globe. It provided this study a good sense of the health issues that will face humanitarian actors assisting North Korean migrants. The two main issues are acute malnutrition and a drug resistant outbreak of tuberculosis.

The resource this study uses to determine the internationally recognized standards for providing aid to dislocated civilians (DCs) is The *Sphere Project Handbook*. The United Nations approved the *Sphere Project Handbook* as its official standard for providing humanitarian assistance. United Nations OCHA used the Sphere Project standards in its response to Haiti.[1]

Two sources identify weaknesses in the North Korean infrastructure that will help understand the difficulty of moving humanitarian assistance around the country. "Coastal cities, port activities and logistic constraints in a socialist developing country: The case of North Korea" published in Transport Reviews and "Gravity model in the Korean

19

Highways" published by Boston University demonstrate the weaknesses of overland transportation in North Korea.

United States Service and Joint Doctrine

The literature that answers the second research question is what United States joint and service doctrine directs the types of activities and operations United States civil affairs forces would conduct in a humanitarian crisis. This paper will survey civil affairs doctrine, civil military operations doctrine, and humanitarian assistance doctrine.

There is joint, navy, and Marine Corps doctrine for humanitarian assistance and civil military operations. Several Joint Publications (JP) cover humanitarian response and civil affairs operations. JP 3-29 *Foreign Humanitarian Assistance* describes the role of United States military forces in a response to a humanitarian crisis in broad terms. JP 3-57 *Civil Military Operations* details CMO for the military and explains in detail the role of civil affairs. The Air Force has Air Force Doctrine Documents (AFDD) for *Military Operations Other Than War and Health Services* that direct the Air Force in its responsibilities for Foreign Humanitarian Assistance, but not a specific AFDD for either civil military operations or humanitarian assistance.

The Army is the only service to have doctrine specific to civil affairs operations. The Army just released a new manual, FM 3-57, *Civil Affairs Operations* in October 2011. FM 3-57 is the only manual that delineates activities specific to civil affairs. Current joint and service doctrine will serve as the foundation for what niche role United States civil affairs forces could serve in a large-scale crisis.

Case Studies

The literature that answers the last secondary research question on what case studies highlight historical uses for civil affairs forces in a large-scale disaster. The Congressional Research Service is the greatest resource for humanitarian response reports to help with researching what case studies share similarities with a humanitarian crisis on the Korean peninsula. A large-scale disaster that employed a significant civil affairs force and illustrated the use of civil affairs in a United States response to a humanitarian crisis was the 2010 Haiti Earthquake.

The most significant literature is an unclassified report released by the 98th civil affairs Battalion that detailed their efforts during Operation Unified Response in Haiti. Additionally, Major Patrick Blakenship published "Into Haiti" in *Special Warfare Magazine* on the United States civil affairs response in Haiti. Another resource that does extensive analysis into the planning and issues related to IDPs and IDP camps is a study by Mark Schuller entitled "Haiti's Disaster after the Disaster: The IDP camps and Cholera." The case study should highlight common issues in responding to a disaster on the same scale as the collapse of the North Korean Regime will likely be.

While each humanitarian crisis is the outcome of a different situation whether it is a tsunami, an earthquake, or the collapse of a repressive regime, many of the issues that arise from both natural and man-made disasters are the same. The case study and issues likely to stem from a collapse of the North Korean Regime include IDPs, humanitarian relief of food and water, and the reconstruction of essential services. The impending crisis on the Korean peninsula will require many of the same response mechanisms the United States military used in the 2010 Haiti earthquake.

Gaps in the Record

Current literature on a possible North Korean collapse focuses on the possibility of the collapse itself. Much of the literature attempts to speculate on how North Korea will collapse and whether it will be a soft landing or a hard landing. Some of the other literature focuses on whether North Korea will begin some reforms prior to the collapse to assist in ensuring there is a soft landing versus a hard landing.

One of the largest collections of literature on a post-collapse response to North Korea focuses on the economic costs of a North Korean collapse. The economic studies focus on how South Korea and its allies will fund a post-collapse North Korea or a possible unification. The next largest group of literature concerning how the international community should respond to a North Korean collapse focuses on consequence management and securing North Korea's suspected nuclear capability. The research in this thesis will help fill the gap on a humanitarian response to a North Korean collapse. This paper will be the first research into the use of United States civil affairs in response to the humanitarian crisis that will follow the collapse of the North Korean regime.

Significance of Thesis in Relation to Existing Literature

Very little literature exists on the use of United States military capabilities to assist South Koreans manage the collapse of the North Korean regime. The analysis and recommendations of this study should assist military staffs prepare for the impending collapse of the North Korean. The results of this study will be particularly useful for special operations planners. Additionally, this study will help define the role of United States civil affairs forces in other humanitarian crises or disaster response missions. An understanding of issues CA will likely face will help the units develop mission specific

training plans.

----

[1]The Sphere Project, *Sphere Project Handbook: Humanitarian Charter and Minimum Standards in Humanitarian Response*, 3rd ed. (United Kingdom: Practical Action Publishing, 2011), 11.

CHAPTER 3

RESEARCH METHODOLOGY

This study will use a qualitative method to analyze the research and data gathered from the literature on the topic. The research determining the scope of the problem is from economic papers and humanitarian journals. The doctrinal use of United States civil affairs forces derives from United States joint and service doctrine. The historical case for the use of United States military, particularly civil affairs, in the response to a large-scale disaster is from military articles and congressional reports on the 2010 Haiti earthquake. This study will analyze data, assess trends, and make a recommendation for the use of United States civil affairs forces.

Internationally Recognized Standards for Handling Dislocated Civilians or Internally Displaced Persons: Sphere Project

The United Nations uses two main references as guidelines for dislocated civilians and humanitarian standards in handling DCs. The first is "Guiding Principles on Internal Displacement" by Walter Kalin, which outlines basic principles for the treatment of dislocated civilians and internally displaced persons (IDPs)[1] The American Society for International Law initially published the paper and the United Nations later approved the principles outlined in the paper. The principles are a legal guide for the general legal treatment of IDPs, but do not have any specifics on handling of IDPs. The second resource is the *Sphere Project Handbook* that is subtitled a *Humanitarian Charter and Minimum Standards in Humanitarian Response*. The United Nations Office for the Coordination of Humanitarian Affairs (United Nations OCHA) uses the Sphere

24

Handbook as a minimum standard for providing humanitarian assistance. The following

quote is from the *Sphere Project Handbook* on how the project came to fruition:

> The Sphere Project–or 'Sphere'–was initiated in 1997 by a group of
> humanitarian non-governmental organizations (NGOs) and the
> International Red Cross and Red Crescent Movement. Their aim was to
> improve the quality of their actions during disaster response and to be held
> accountable for them. They based Sphere's philosophy on two core
> beliefs: first, that those affected by disaster or conflict have a right to life
> with dignity and, therefore, a right to assistance; and second, that all
> possible steps should be taken to alleviate human suffering arising out of
> disaster or conflict.[2]

This study will use the Sphere Project for the minimum standards to determine the

requirements that will provide a planning guideline on the scope of the problem facing

South Korea and its allies. The sphere standards will help measure land requirements,

sustainment requirements, and should help give an idea for securing camps for IDPs or

DCs.

Any discussion on the handling of dislocated civilians or internally displaced

civilians must be in line with internationally accepted standards. This study will use

Kalin's *Guiding Principles* and the *Sphere Project Handbook* as its basis while

conducting analysis to the needs that the North Korean migrants will have following the

collapse of the North Korean Regime.

<u>Scope of the Disaster</u>

To answer the first secondary question, pertaining to the scope of the

humanitarian crisis, this study will use qualitative data gleaned from other academic

works that use economic models to determine the number of IDPs that would migrate

after regime collapse as well as the amount of space and basic needs each displaced

person will need. This paper will use data from current studies concerning the need to for

25

humanitarian assistance, particularly food and medical, in North Korea. Additionally, other qualitative studies will determine how much infrastructure repair North Korea will require following the collapse of the Regime.

This study will estimate the amount of migration that would follow a collapse of the North Korean regime to scope the size of the disaster. The amount of Dislocated Civilians (DCs) will have a massive impact on the operations of South Korea and its allies. A crisis that includes a large number of migrants and DCs comes with other attendant issues such as security, controlling the flow of people, space for camps, water, food, sanitation, disease, and legal protections.

The next problem in the crisis will be the humanitarian aid issues that will arise after the collapse of the North Korean regime. The DPRK is already suffering a food shortage crisis. North Korea receives 45 percent of its food from China alone, and there is still a 414, 000 metric ton food deficit.[3] In addition to chronic and acute malnutrition health issues, North Korea has had an outbreak of drug resistant tuberculosis. The current life expectancy of a North Korean that contracts tuberculosis is currently four years.[4] South Korea and its allies will have to assess the environment, detect health and humanitarian issues, organize among international partners, and decide how the group will approach each issue.

The third aspect of the humanitarian crisis following the collapse of the North Korean Regime will be the infrastructure requirements that the international community will have to repair. CA, as member of the military, does not conduct development for needs based purposes. However, under the auspices of Defense Security Cooperation, United States code authorizes the military to build infrastructure for humanitarian or disaster relief purposes.[5] The United States military will play a role in some infrastructure improvement early in the response repairing or build new essential services. United States civil affairs forces will play a large part of the United States military's immediate response.

The analysis of those three aspects of the humanitarian crisis will develop a clearer picture of the operational environment the Republic of Korea and its allies will face. The analysis should also include an expected end state level of IDPs transitioned to IGOs and NGOs, level of stabilization of malnutrition and health concerns, and a level of essential services. Developing a baseline level will help determine a transition of military activities to other actors and will help frame a level of effort the crisis will require.

There is a wide range of literature speculating on how many Koreans will try to migrate following a collapse of the North Korean regime. The numbers range from 800,000 in Stares and Wit's "Preparing for Sudden Change in North Korea"[6] up to five million over 10 years in Seung Mo Choi's economic modeling on the impacts of reunification.[7] Another issue is whether the migrating population will go to China or go to South Korea. Stares and Wit contend that a majority of the defectors will head towards China following a collapse of the North Korean Regime.[8] Choi believes that most of the migrants will flow to South Korea following a collapse of the North Korean Regime due to familial ties and the percentage of migration that flows South will increase over time as North Koreans come to understand the economic opportunities in the South.[9]

One of the reasons Stares and Wit indicate a northern migration towards China is the heavily mined DMZ and the danger it would present to migration. However, there are indicators and trends of current defections to indicate that North Koreans could find routes across the DMZ shortly after a collapse. Tara O shows a rapid increase in the

number of defectors from North Korea to South Korea over the last decade.[10]

Table 1.   North Korean Defectors to South Korea

Year	Prior to 1990	1990	1991	1992	1993	1994	1995	1996	1997	1998	1999
Number	670	9	9	8	8	52	41	56	85	72	148

Year	2000	2001	2002	2003	2004	2005	2006	2007	2008	2009	2010
Number	312	583	1,139	1,281	1,894	1,387	2,018	2,544	2,809	2,927	2,376

Source: Tara O, "The Integration of North Korean Defectors in South Korea: Problems and Prospects," *International Journal of Korean Studies* 15, no. 2 (June 2011): 151-169. Table shows the rapid increase in defections at the turn of the millennia.

Table 1 shows two things in the numbers. The first supports this study's

contention and that of Andrew Scobell that North Korean control measures have begun to

erode. Additionally, the data shows that North Koreans are not overly frightened at the

prospect of the DMZ. North Koreans are willing to take the risk to approach and bribe

North Korean border guards to help them cross the DMZ safely and defect to South

Korea.[11] In the decade spanning 2001 to 2010, nearly 20,000 North Koreans crossed the

DMZ into South Korea.

This study is going to use the numbers produced by Seung Mo Choi's economic

study as the framework for most likely and most extreme scenarios to frame the

migration problem South Korea and its allies will face following a collapse of the North

Korean regime. This study will use those numbers for a few reasons. First, Choi used a

quantitative analysis to develop models for North Korean migration. Second, Choi shows migration over time for ten years allowing better analysis of the level of the crisis. Third, this study contends North Koreans are more willing than many believe to cross the DMZ.

The Choi study used mathematical formulas based on food distribution and the current economic divide to try to make a determination on how many North Koreans would migrate south along with assumptions garnered by looking at trends from East German to West German Migration. The end state for Choi is to determine the economic impact of migration on reunification. Choi's model provides this study an expected number of DCs after the collapse of the North Korean regime. The weakness of the mathematical model is that it produces a steady rate of migration over 10 years. The result of his modeling was a two percent migration rate over ten years.[12] Choi's calculation puts North Korean migration up to 4.8 million. When Choi calculated for an "unlikely-to-occur upper bound,"[13] his calculations yielded a five percent migration rate over ten years or 11.9 million migrants over ten years. This study is going to use the base case, probable case, of two percent.

Using Choi's rate, there will be 480,000 migrants moving to South Korea each year. The table below shows the effects the base and upper bound migration would have on populations both north and south of the border. The quick drop-off in the upper bound case for migration is a visual that translates into numbers of people migrating to South Korea that will require care and feeding.

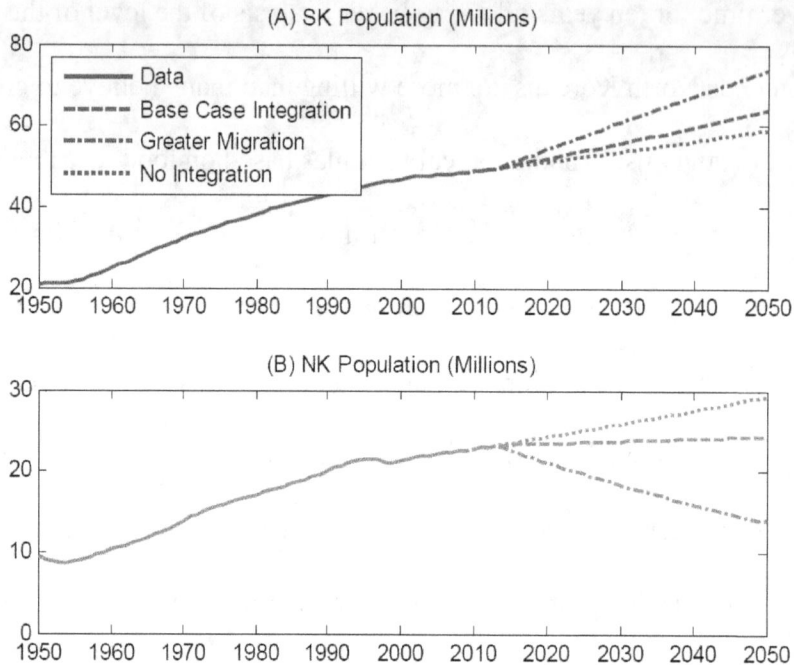

Figure 2.   Post Collapse Migration Rates and the Effects on North and South Korean
Populations
Source: Seung Mo Choi, "Economic Impacts of Reunifications in Germany and Korea,"
Washington State School of Economics, December 2011, 29.

Managing the movement of nearly a half a million dislocated civilians presents a

daunting task. The expected amount of migration of 480,000 is the equivalent of Kansas

City's population moving across the border requiring care and feeding.[14] The upper

bound case would be the equivalent of Dallas, Texas migrating to South Korea.[15] That

number of dislocated civilians will require a significant response from the international

community.

<u>Joint and Service Doctrine</u>

To answer the next secondary research question, pertaining to the United States

doctrine that directs United States forces or civil affairs forces to conduct humanitarian assistance missions, the paper will use a qualitative analysis of United States doctrine, both joint and service, to determine United States doctrinal capabilities to assist in a humanitarian response. Joint Doctrine as well as each service doctrine dictates what a joint force or service component is capable of providing in a disaster response scenario.

The Air Force and Marine Corps published some doctrine detailing the role of forces in humanitarian assistance roles or civil military operations. The two AFDDs that explain the role of the Air Force in CMO or humanitarian assistance are AFDD 2-3, *Military Operations Other Than War* and AFDD 2-4.2, *Health Services*. The Air Force establishes three main roles in a humanitarian response, but only in broad terms. The three roles are airlift of humanitarian supplies, construction support, and health care. The Air Force does not designate a force that conducts humanitarian missions. This study will only consider Air Force Doctrine in context of a larger United States military response, but not specifics of the role civil affairs will play.

The Marine Corps has MCWP 3-33.1 *Marine Air-Ground Task Force Civil Military Operations* that outlines Marine doctrine in CMO and a humanitarian response. The Marine Corps does have a reserve force that is designated as a civil affairs force and will be considered at the time of recommendations. The MCWP is broad in its scope and does not contain specifics on CMO or humanitarian assistance. Additionally, the Marine Corps relied heavily on Joint and Army Doctrine to develop its manual.

Joint doctrine is usually less detailed than service doctrine. This study is going to focus on the tasks outlined in JP 2-29 *Foreign Humanitarian Assistance* and JP 3-57 *Civil Military Operations*. Joint Doctrine is the foundation this study will use to determine the overall tasks civil affairs will conduct in a response to the humanitarian crisis that will

31

follow the collapse of the North Korean Regime. However, this study is going to focus on Army doctrine for more specifics on civil affairs capabilities and doctrinal tasks. FM 3-37 *Civil Affairs Operations* will give more clarity to the tasks specified for United States civil affairs forces. Currently, the United States Army is the only service to specifically train, man, and equip specialized civil affairs units.[16]

This study will analyze joint and service doctrine to determine what specific activities United States civil affairs is capable of conducting or best suited to conduct in coordination with host nation, interagency, intergovernmental, and non-governmental actors in the humanitarian crisis that will follow the collapse of the North Korean Regime.

Haiti Case Study

The last secondary question, examines the role of the United States military and United States civil affairs in past humanitarian crisis response scenarios. This paper will use the Haiti earthquake in 2010 as a case study for the use of United States civil affairs in a large-scale humanitarian response. This study will use the response to the 2010 earthquake in Haiti for several reasons.

The United States military response involved a significant civil affairs presence as part of the response.[17] SOCOM deployed the entire 98th Civil Affairs Battalion to Haiti to assist in the United States response.[18] The large amount of civil affairs involved and the many roles played by the 98th will serve as anecdotal support to the doctrinal use of civil affairs in a large-scale humanitarian response.

Haiti also was similar in scale to the situation humanitarian actors will face in North Korea in terms of DCs, food aid, dilapidated or non-existent infrastructure, and health issues. Haiti had nearly 1.5 million people lose their homes in the earthquake. United Nations OCHA and other humanitarian organizations had to find locations and design camps to accommodate the dislocated civilians.[19] United Nations OCHA mandated the use of the *Guiding Principles* and the *Sphere Project Handbook* to determine minimum standards.[20] The United States military in coordination with civilian aid agencies had a responsibility to deliver aid to a large dislocated populace. The health issues that faced dislocated civilians in DC camps in Haiti will be similar to those faced by United States civil affairs in Korea. The required response in Haiti forced several disparate organizations to work in a coordinated manner. The humanitarian response to the collapse of the North Korean regime will require a large response with coordination issues similar to those in Haiti. The case study will be effective in answering the last secondary question due to similar scopes of the humanitarian issues at hand even if the circumstances and politics are different.

The analysis in this study will lead to recommendations for United States civil affairs as a response to a humanitarian crisis after the fall of the North Korean Regime. The humanitarian crisis after the fall of North Korea will be a crisis of magnitude. United States joint and service doctrine prescribes critical HA activities as part of a crisis response. The Haiti case study will serve as a historical reference and provide lessons learned from civil affairs participation in an earlier humanitarian crisis of magnitude. The recommendations derived from the analysis in chapter four will assist future planners in preparing for the collapse of the North Korean regime.

[1]Walter Kälin, "Guiding Principles on Internal Displacement," *Studies in Transnational Legal Policy.* No 38 (2008), 2.

[2]The Sphere Project, 4.

[3]Justin McCury, "No End in Sight for North Korea's Malnutrition Crisis," *The Lance.* 379, no. 18 (February 2012): 602.

[4]North Korea struggling with tuberculosis outbreak - South paper," *BBC Monitoring International Reports,* 12 November 2011, *Academic OneFile.* http://go.galegroup.com/ps/i.do?id=GALE%7CA272354375&v=2.1&u=97mwrlib&it=r &p=AONE&sw=w (accessed 18 April 2012).

[5]Department of Defense Directive 2205.02, *Humanitarian and Civic Assistance (HCA) Activities,* 2 December 2008, 23.

[6]Paul B. Stares and Joel S. Wit. "Preparing for Sudden Change in North Korea," *Council on Foreign Relations* Special Report, no. 4 (January 2009), 23.

[7]Seung Mo Choi, *Economic Impacts of Reunifications in Germany and Korea.* Washington State School of Economics, December 2011, 36.

[8]Stares and Wit. "Preparing for Sudden Change in North Korea," 24.

[9]Choi, *Economic Impacts of Reunifications in Germany and Korea,* 38.

[10]O, "The Integration of North Korean Defectors in South Korea: Problems and Prospects," *International Journal of Korean Studies* 15, no. 2 (June 2011): 155.

[11]Ibid., 156.

[12]Choi, *Economic Impacts of Reunifications in Germany and Korea,* 28.

[13]Ibid., 36.

[14]United States Census Bureau, http://quickfacts.census.gov/qfd/states/ 29/2938000.html. (accessed 12 April 2012).

[15]United States Census Bureau, http://quickfacts.census.gov/qfd/states/ 48/4819000.html. (accessed 12 April 2012).

[16]United States Department of the Army, FM 3-57, *Civil Affairs Operations* (Fort Bragg: Department of the Army, 2011), 2-1.

[17]Rhoda Margesson, *Haiti Earthquake: Crisis and Response* (Washington, DC: Congressional Research Service, 2010), 15.

[18]Patric Blakenship, "Into Haiti." *Special Warfare Magazine* (September-October 2010): 25.

[19]Mark Schuller, "Haiti's Disaster after the Disaster: The IDP Camps and Cholera," *The Journal of Humanitarian Assistance* (December 2011): 1.

[20]Schuller, "Haiti's Disaster after the Disaster: The IDP Camps and Cholera," 2.

CHAPTER 4

ANALYSIS

The purpose of this paper is to show there is a niche role for United States civil affairs forces in a humanitarian crisis following the collapse of the North Korean regime. In order to determine what that niche role is likely to be, this chapter will examine the problem facing humanitarian actors, United States doctrine, and a case study to conduct the analysis. Analyzing the scope of a post-collapse disaster will demonstrate the myriad of problems a humanitarian response will address. A study of joint and service doctrine as it relates to humanitarian assistance and civil affairs operations will outline the specific tasks and capabilities civil affairs is directed to provide. A case study of the 2010 Haiti earthquake will demonstrate the historic use of civil affairs in a large-scale humanitarian response. The analysis in this chapter will provide the basis for recommending a possible niche roll for civil affairs post-collapse Korea humanitarian response.

Scope of a Post Collapse Disaster

Internally Displaced Persons and Dislocated Civilians

The care and feeding of 480,000 dislocated civilians is a humanitarian crisis of magnitude. Humanitarian actors will have to provide shelter, food, and medical assistance to the DCs. The international community has a responsibility to provide those resources in a responsible way. Providing the amount of resources required will take a coordinated effort among many partners. Civil affairs have a role to play in that humanitarian response.

DC Camps and Related Issues

The issue of dislocated civilians is both a legally and physically complicated matter. The legal and humanitarian frameworks that shape the standard for the *Sphere Project Handbook* build a group of principles for the care and housing of all people. The Sphere Project defines that first principle of adequate housing as "sufficient space and protection from cold, damp, heat, rain, wind or other threats to health, including structural hazards and disease vectors."[1] The first principle of adequate housing will be the basis for the minimal requirements to house dislocated civilians.

United States civil affairs are not likely to get involved in long term solutions for North Korean migration, but will likely establish temporary shelters in the immediate aftermath of the North Korean regime's collapse. Even temporary shelters have minimal standards to which humanitarian actors must adhere. The first standard to consider is the slope of a possible DC camp. Any site must have an appropriate slope to facilitate proper drainage. The site must have no less than a one percent grade to ensure no standing water and no more than a five percent grade to ensure the flow of water is not too fast.[2] Another planning consideration that will affect site selection is proximity to a breeding site for vector born diseases.[3] Any camp should be located at least one to two kilometers upwind of any breeding site. The geography of Korea presents challenges when selecting sites that meet grade and vector born disease requirements. Figure 3 below shows the steep topography of Korea around the DMZ. The terrain close to the DMZ is a series of rugged ridgelines and low valleys used for rice farming. The canalized terrain presents difficulties for grade requirements, and the probability of breeding sites in the low-lying farm areas creates difficulties in reducing risks to vector born diseases. Besides the difficulties with terrain, the sheer space consideration required for the large number of

expected DCs present other difficulties.

The second consideration is the total amount of space required. The *Sphere Project Handbook* sets 45 square meters per person as the standard for temporary camps.[4] The *Sphere Project Handbook* requires 21.6 million square meters or 500 football fields to house 480,000 DCs temporarily. In addition to living space, the *Sphere Project Handbook* calls for another 30 square meters per person of communal space for latrines, cooking and eating areas, and meeting areas.[5] Communal spaces will require an additional 4.4 million square meters or an additional 340 football fields. The last space using requirements are fire safety measures. The *Sphere Project Handbook* requires a 30 meter fire break between every 300 meters of built up space and a minimum of two meters between every shelter.[6] The amount of dislocated civilians expected in the scenario will require approximately 1000 football fields of space to provide the minimum requirements by international standards.

Besides space, people need food and water provided to internationally accepted standards.[7] North Korean people are already suffering from both chronic and acute malnutrition. How much food will South Korea and its allies need to provide? The food shortage in North Korea last year was 414,000 tons.[8] The *Sphere Project Handbook* does not offer a simple answer to food requirements per day. The food requirement is based on the size, age, sex, and activity level of each individual's dietary requirement. The *Sphere Project Handbook* does not address the issue of chronic or acute malnutrition, but humanitarian actors will have to make adjustments to food aid to many North Koreans.[9] One of the issues the *Sphere Project Handbook* does raise is providing dried food goods like Meals Ready to Eat (MREs) to vulnerable people. Dried goods are easy to steal and may put DCs at further risk from attack.[10] The *Sphere Project Handbook* does list specific requirements for water per person per day. The *Sphere Project Handbook* lists 7.5 to 15 liters per day per person as the standard for water. At 10 liters per day, that would mean providing the equivalent of 9.6 million bottles or 73,000 tons of water every day to dislocated civilians. The government of South Korea, its allies, and international governmental organizations need to identify all food and water storage areas in North Korea and prepare stores of food and water in South Korea for the eventual humanitarian response.

Humanitarian actors must be prepared to address health concerns among the North Korean people. Aside from chronic malnutrition, there is currently an outbreak of drug resistant tuberculosis in North Korea.[11] Aid workers, to include the United States military, need to prepare to isolate infected people for treatment to limit the spread of the disease. Additionally, humanitarian actors will have to ensure proper sanitation in the design of DC camps as well as give classes for sanitation. Illnesses caused by poor sanitation often cause significant health problems in camps.[12]

Typically, IGOs, NGOs, and government aid organizations will not have the ability to move needed supplies to what could be nearly 1000 camps and will use the military's "unmatched capabilities in logistics, command and control, communications, and mobility."[13] The South Korean and United States militaries will have a requirement to assist in the transportation and distribution of humanitarian relief supplies. Both militaries are very adept at logistic management. The interaction between the South Korean and United States militaries with civilian organizations will require a system to facilitate communication and prioritization. The United Nations and other civilian organizations always base the priority of aid on need. Only professionally assessed medical needs will drive the priority of assistance.[14] The military will have to provide some liaisons with United Nations OCHA and civilian aid organizations to synchronize efforts and ensure proper distribution of humanitarian supplies based on humanitarian principles.

The challenges of moving logistics across the DMZ or around the southern portion of North Korea will be formidable. The sheer number of DCs and the logistics requirement to support the camps will be a major challenge for the international community to manage which deficiencies in North Korean infrastructure only make harder. The DMZ is the most heavily mined border in the world, and no public roads connect the South to the north.[15]

The challenges of distribution only begin once relief aid makes it to North Korea. North Korea has a limited road network capable of transporting significant amounts of resources. "Despite the recent reforms and the growth of trade, the development of North Korea is confronted to the weaknesses of the transport system and inland logistics."[16] North Korea only has 724 kilometers of paved road or 6.2 percent of its total road networks.[17] Most of the paved roads run from North Korea's main ports, Nampo and Sariwon, to Pyongyang or from China to its industrial centers in the North.[18] Travel to any other part of North Korea by road is more difficult. North Korea attempts to make up the difference by shipping supplies by rail. The rail system has its own issues as well. North Korea is using steam engines left from the Japanese occupation before World War II. Despite abundant coal in North Korea, North Korea uses second hand tires to fuel their locomotive steam engines due to inefficiencies mining and processing coal.[19]

South Korea, its allies, and civilian aid agencies will face a monumental task overcoming systemic failures in the North Korean logistics infrastructure to ensure they are able to deliver aid to outlying regions. Humanitarian actors will have to assess weaknesses in the infrastructure, prioritize reconstruction efforts, and distribute responsibility based on capability. South Korea, the United States, OCHA, and civilian aid agencies must ensure effective coordination to ensure proper distribution.

The problem facing humanitarian actors in a response to the humanitarian crisis following the collapse of the North Korean Regime is how to manage a half million dislocated civilians, provide food, water, and health assistance, deliver aid to outlying regions in an effort to relieve human suffering and stabilize the Korean Peninsula. The scope of the problem will require a coordinated effort of the South Korean Government, the United States Interagency, intergovernmental organizations, and non-governmental organizations. United States civil affairs has a unique capability that will provide assistance in this larger effort.

Humanitarian Assistance and Civil Affairs Doctrine

This study will examine joint and service doctrine to determine what tasks doctrine designates civil to conduct. JP 3-29 *Foreign Humanitarian Assistance* is the base doctrine for defense involvement in humanitarian operations. This paper will primarily refer to JP 3-57 *Civil Affairs Operations* to determine the specific tasks doctrine directs civil affairs to conduct in a humanitarian crisis.

JP 3-29 *Foreign Humanitarian Assistance* is the primary joint doctrine that defines roles and responsibilities in humanitarian assistance missions. JP 3-29 discusses the roles and responsibilities of different military and civilian organizations across several aspects of a humanitarian response. The aspects include deployment, assessment, command and control, intelligence, and sustainment among the twenty aspects the JP lists.[20] Additionally, JP 3-29 is a guide, in broad terms, on planning and executing foreign humanitarian operations. JP 3-29 is the base doctrine for humanitarian assistance, but does not list specific tasks for civil affairs in a humanitarian response.

FM 3-57 *Civil Affairs Operations* lists specific tasks that United States civil affairs forces will need to conduct as part of a humanitarian response following an event like the collapse of the North Korean Regime. According to FM 3-57, civil affairs has five core tasks. Those core tasks are Populace and Resources Control (PRC), Foreign

Humanitarian Assistance (FHA), Civil Information Management (CIM), Nation

Assistance (NA), and Support to Civil Administration (SCA). FM 3-57 breaks down each

core task into subtasks civil affairs can conduct to achieve the mission. Figure 4

demonstrates civil affairs organizations as the base that conducts the five pillars, or civil

affairs core tasks, to support civil affairs operations and mission requirements. Civil

Affairs Operations (CAO) is an integral part of the Army's Unified Land Operations and

the joint force's Unified Action.

Figure 4.   Civil Affairs Core Tasks in support of Unified Action

Source. United States Department of the Army, FM 3-57, *Civil Affairs Operations* (Fort
Bragg: Department of the Army, 2011), 1-4.

Nested within the civil affairs core tasks are the roles civil affairs will play as a part of the United States military's efforts in a humanitarian response following the collapse of the North Korean regime. Those specific tasks will help ensure civil affairs are not duplicating capabilities and synchronize their efforts with other Joint, Interagency, Intergovernmental, and Multinational (JIIM) actors.

Populace and Resource Control

Large numbers of dislocated civilians is one of the biggest issues facing humanitarian actors following the collapse of the North Korean Regime. The civil affairs core task of Populace and Resource Control (PRC) directly addresses the DC issue. "The PRC operation consists of two distinct, yet linked, components: populace control and resources control."[21] Population control, more than resource control, relates directly to the dislocated civilian problem. FM 3-57 defines population control as a task that "provides security for the populace, mobilizes human resources, denies enemy access to the population, and detects and reduces the effectiveness of enemy agents."[22] The two forms of populace control are Noncombatant Evacuation Operations and Dislocated Civilian Operations. FM 3-57 directs civil affairs to assist in managing DC operations for the military. FM 3-57 goes on to list the categories of dislocated civilians and the legal and political considerations the international community assigned to each category.

Army Doctrine assigns civil affairs very specific responsibilities during DC operations. These tasks are:

1. Identifying or evaluating existing HN and international community DC plans and operations.

44

2. Advising on DC control measures that would effectively support the military

   operation.

3. Advising on how to implement DC control measures.

4. Publicizing control measures among Indigenous Populations and Institutions

   (IPI).

5. Assessing MOEs.

6. Participating in the execution of selected DC operations as needed or directed

   and in coordination with the internationally mandated organizations (for

   example, UNHCR, Office for the Coordination of Humanitarian Affairs, and

   the ICRC) for their care.

7. Assisting in arbitration of problems arising from implementation of DC control

   measures.[23]

The specific tasks directing civil affairs towards a discreet set of actions in FM 3-57 will assist in both the planning and execution phases of DC operations. The effort will require consulting with IGOs and NGOs as well as detailed planning with the government of South Korea.

FM 3-57 lists securing commodities (food and fuel) storage facilities, implementing commodities rationing, securing property rights, and protecting key civil infrastructure and sites as tasks for resource control operations. Resource control does not relate as directly to the largest humanitarian issue following the collapse of the North Korean regime, but several elements of resource control will be important to a post collapse humanitarian response. Resources that will be important to identify and secure for humanitarian purposes is property, food, water, and medicine.

The main role that United States civil affairs could play in coordination with its South Korean counterparts is securing North Korean food stores before thieves empty what food does exist in North Korea. "Securing existing harvest storage facilities to prevent spoilage and looting of harvested crops" is a specific task doctrine directs civil affairs to conduct.[24] The initial humanitarian response is going to depend on resources already in North Korea or poised in South Korea near the DMZ. North Korea's current malnutrition issues and likely migration will both ensure a need for food aid and put current North Korean food stores at risk. Prudence dictates South Korea and its allies prepare to locate and secure North Korean food stores immediately after the collapse of the North Korean Regime.

Another resource control task identified for civil affairs to conduct is "Establishing procedures to resolve property rights for land."[25] If North Korean migrants could be convinced to return home, South Korea and its allies will have to develop a system to guarantee property rights for North Koreans giving them a place to return. Resource control is a task listed in civil affairs doctrine. The task of identifying and developing a system to ensure property rights for North Koreans will belong to the government of South Korea.[26] Civil affairs forces may play a role in training the South Korean Army on resource control tasks as part of a combined exercise focused on preparing for the humanitarian issues South Korea will face after a collapse of North Korea.

Foreign Humanitarian Assistance

Foreign Humanitarian Assistance (FHA) is a civil affairs core task that directs civil affairs to operate as a humanitarian actor. FM 3-57 defines FHA as "programs conducted to relieve or reduce the results of natural or man-made disasters or other endemic conditions, such as human pain, disease, hunger, or need that might present a serious threat to life or that can result in great damage to or loss of property."[27] Typically, United States military assistance in a humanitarian crisis is limited in scope and duration.[28] The United States Agency for International Development's (USAID) Office of Foreign Disaster Assistance (OFDA) is the primary agency for a United States response to a natural or manmade disaster. Responding to a humanitarian crisis is an inherently complex operation requiring interagency coordination.[29]

FM 3-57 directs civil affairs to conduct the following tasks in support of a commander's humanitarian mission:

1. Participate in the preparation and review of contingency plans that address assisting USG agencies, IGOs, HN agencies, and NGOs to support FHA.

2. Monitor all FHA operations for compliance with applicable laws, agreements, treaties, and contracts.

3. Review guidance from the GCC regarding FHA operations in TSCPs, FHA and disaster relief plans, and foreign consequence management plans.

4. Incorporate FHA assessment and FHA training into TSCPs.

5. Assess the environment in which U.S. forces will conduct FHA operations, including the—

   a. Political situation.

   b. Physical boundaries of the area.

   c. Potential threat to forces.

   d. Global visibility of the situation.

e. Media interest climate for FHA operations.

6. Confirm and validate the HN's ability to manage HA in the AO.

7. Establish a CMOC to coordinate and synchronize CAO and CMO efforts with interagency and multinational HA efforts in the AO.[30]

Civil affairs should focus on critical FHA tasks to prepare for a humanitarian crisis following a collapse of the North Korean regime. The first task for civil affairs is to integrate its planning and execution efforts with multinational, interagency, and intergovernmental partners. United States forces as well as other humanitarian actors will support the South Korean government and its military forces as the sovereign host nation. The second FHA task is providing immediate food and medical aid to alleviate human suffering. The last FHA task is short-term construction to either provide essential service or to ensure recovery from the disaster.

The United Nations cluster system is the operational framework through which civil affairs will conduct these tasks. This system is the designated method implemented by the United Nations Office of the Coordinator for Humanitarian Affairs (United Nations OCHA) to respond to humanitarian crises.[31] The United Nations cluster system designates IGO or NGO lead agencies for each sector. As an example, the lead for logistics is the World Food Program. All support and requests for support should pass through the World Food Program to ensure that food donors can fill requests for food while ensuring aid organizations distribute food in accordance with international standards.[32] The cluster sectors are health, telecommunications, emergency shelter, nutrition, logistics, protection, sanitation, water and hygiene, education, emergency early recovery, and agriculture. The figure below shows which IGO or NGO OCHA has assigned as lead agency for different sectors during a disaster response. Humanitarian

actors must be capable of coordinating with the host nation and through the United

Nations cluster system based on a quality assessment and good information on the

humanitarian need.

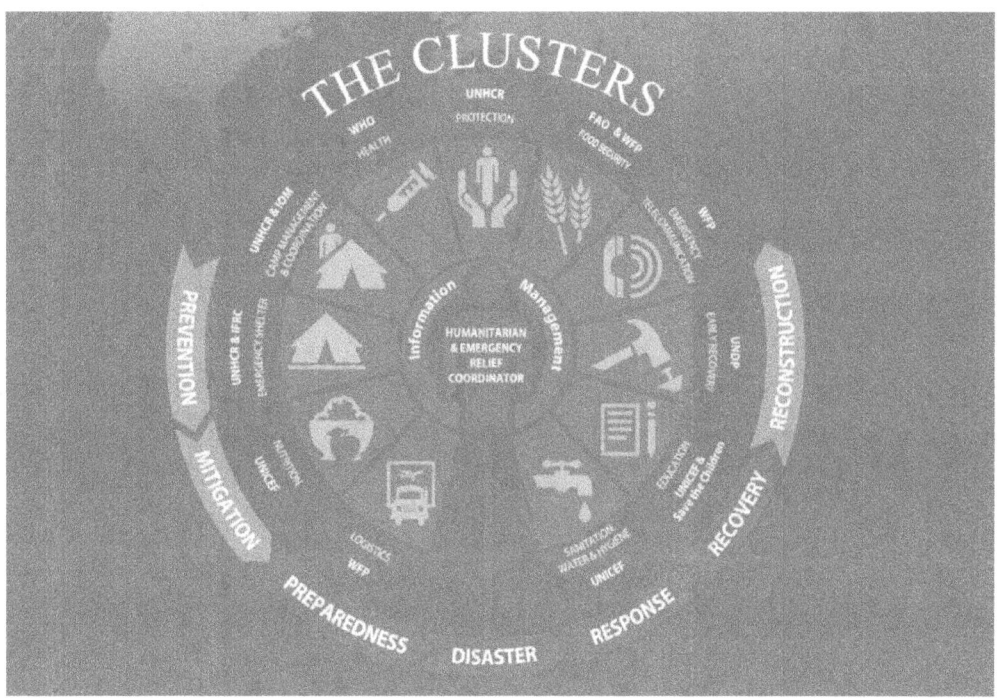

Figure 5.   The United Nations Cluster System

Source. United Nations Office for the Coordination of Humanitarian Affairs, "How are
disaster relief efforts organised? Cluster Approach," http://business.un.org/en/.../
39c87a78-fec9-402e-a434-2c355f24e4f4.pdf (accessed 3 April 2012).

Civil Information Management

The civil affairs core task that directs civil affairs to conduct assessments, develop

the civil picture, and share the information with partners is Civil Information

Management (CIM). FM 3-57 defines CIM as:

> Civil Information Management is the process whereby civil information is
> collected, entered into a central database, and internally fused with the
> supported element, higher HQ, and other USG and DOD agencies, IGOs,
> and NGOs. This process ensures the timely availability of information for
> analysis and the widest possible dissemination of the raw and analyzed
> civil information to military and nonmilitary partners throughout the
> AO.[33]

The civil information management process has six steps: collection, collation,

processing, analysis, production and dissemination.[34] The two key aspects of the CIM

process are conducting rapid and accurate assessments and then ensuring there is a

mechanism to share information with all partners working in the humanitarian response.

Civil affairs units are well suited to conduct timely assessments with their ability

to deploy rapidly and operate in a semi-permissive environment. FM 3-57 directs civil

affairs to conduct civil reconnaissance (CR) to assess the civil environment and collect

civil information. FM 3-57 defines CR as "targeted, planned, and coordinated observation

and evaluation of specific civil aspects of the environment. CR focuses on the civil

component, the elements of which are best represented by the acronym ASCOPE: area,

structures, capabilities, organizations, people, and events."[35] Civil affairs need to

coordinate efforts with their South Korean counterparts, with civilian aid agencies, and

the rest of the joint force.

United States civil affairs forces need to ensure they are disseminating

information to all humanitarian actors. Other actors may not know what information or products civil affairs has collected and produced. Additionally, civil affairs may not anticipate all the requirements civilian humanitarian actors may have. Civil affairs should seek feedback from the organizations that civil affairs previously shared data with to make gradual improvements. Civil affairs forces need to push all their products out to the widest dissemination possible to ensure coordination across humanitarian actors. "Sharing is the cornerstone of CIM and is the hallmark of interagency cooperation."[36] Civil affairs forces should use layered geospatial products using systems like ARC GIS to ensure accurate and clear information for dissemination.

Civil information serves as a tool to assist the military to collaborate with interagency and other civilian counterparts. A broad dissemination of civil data helps reduce duplication or conflicts in the humanitarian space. Civil data, shred through a coordinating cell, assists all relief organizations coordinate efforts.

Developing organizations that coordinate between the JTF and the interagency or intergovernmental organizations like the United Nations cluster system mitigates gaps or overlaps in services.[37] Civil affairs usually develops an organization like a Civil Military Operations Center (CMOC) or a Humanitarian Assistance Coordination Center (HACC) as a central location to coordinate with or share information with the interagency or intergovernmental organizations.[38] The relationships built through operations or coordination centers are essential to ensuring the best input to the CIM process and the best product for civil affairs to share with its interagency and intergovernmental partners.

Nation Assistance

The civil affairs core task of Nation Assistance (NA) is important for United States civil affairs in preparation for a collapse. NA outlines the authorities and some

51

funding civil affairs can use to prepare for a collapse of North Korea. Civil affairs

subtasks covered under NA include Security Assistance (SA), Foreign Internal Defense

(FID), and Humanitarian Civic Action (HCA). The NA tasks will help United States

forces train, equip, and build projects as part of training in preparation for a humanitarian

crisis in a post-collapse North Korea.

Nation Assistance is the task that directs civil affairs forces to train with partners

to increase partner capability or to increase interoperability with partner organizations.

FM 3-57 defines NA as "assistance (other than FHA) rendered to a nation by U.S. forces

within that nation's territory during peacetime, crises or emergencies, or war based on

agreements mutually concluded between the United States and that nation. NA operations

support a host nation by promoting sustainable development and growth of responsive

institutions."[39] Civil affairs must work with South Korean military to identify relative

strengths and weaknesses of forces to ensure proper training and interoperability of both

forces and government agencies.

Nation assistance consists of three sub tasks: SA, FID, and HCA.[40] Foreign

internal defense includes tasks to secure populations. Engagement with South Korean

counterparts while training on FID tasks will help prepare United States and South

Korean forces to conduct humanitarian operations in less secure operating environments.

Through security assistance, United States civil affairs will be able to train the South

Korean military on United States civil affairs tactics, techniques, and procedures.

The advantage humanitarian civic action has over security assistance is funding.

The main purpose of HCA is to train United States and host nation forces on common

skill sets. HCA has funding incidental to the training that can benefit a humanitarian purpose for the population.[41] United States and South Korean soldiers could conduct a joint exercise and HCA money could fund construction of future DC camps or other humanitarian projects that would help prepare for the humanitarian crisis that will follow the collapse of the North Korean regime.

Civil affairs doctrine dictates certain actions during a humanitarian response. Doctrine directs civil affairs to assist with dislocated civilians as a populace control measure. Doctrine indicates civil affairs should identify and secure key resources such as food in the PRC core task. Civil affairs doctrine directs CA to assist the care and feeding of dislocated civilians in compliance with international standards such as those dictated in the *Sphere Project Handbook*.[42] Doctrine instructs United States civil affairs to conduct Civil Information management by conducting civil reconnaissance, analyzing and distributing information through the CIM process, and facilitating JIIM coordination. Nation Assistance directs civil affairs to build host nation military and government capacity. Nation Assistance will be instrumental in preparing for a large-scale disaster.

The 98th Civil Affairs Battalion's activities as part of the United States military response to the 2010 Haiti earthquake demonstrate the tasks assigned to civil affairs by doctrine. The Haiti earthquake is a good case study for the use of Civil Affairs in a humanitarian crisis. The lessons learned in Haiti will be useful in planning for other large magnitude humanitarian responses.

2010 Haiti Earthquake Case Study

The 2010 Haiti earthquake was a large-scale disaster that caught the attention of the American people and triggered a massive United States response. 12 January 2010 a 7.0 magnitude earthquake struck off the coast of Port-au-Prince, the capital of Haiti, killing 300,000, destroying most of the infrastructure in and around Port-au-Prince, and effectively eliminating the national government.[43] The Haiti earthquake was the first large scale use of United States civil affairs forces in a disaster response. United States Special Operations Command (SOCOM) sent an entire civil affairs battalion to assist in the earthquake response in Haiti. The 98th Civil Affairs Battalion (A) had Soldiers in Haiti within twenty-four hours of the earthquake striking Port-au-Prince.[44]

The impending humanitarian crisis in a post-collapse North Korea may differ in causation from Haiti, but there are many similarities to the outcomes of both disasters. Both crises are large-scale disasters with large numbers of dislocated civilians. There were over one million in Haiti and a half million expected in Korea.[45] Humanitarian actors will face many of the same challenges of providing food, water, and health assistance to a dislocated populace. The collapse of the North Korean regime will leave North Korea an ungoverned space without the intervention of other nations or the United Nations. The 2010 Haiti earthquake killed many government leaders and the government was not able to assist its people and temporarily required the intervention of the United Nations.[46] The logistical challenge of moving aid from the coast to more remote areas exists in both an impending crisis in North Korea and the 2010 Haiti earthquake. North Korea lacks road infrastructure away from ports or the capital city, and the 2010 Haiti earthquake further damaged Haiti's already dilapidated infrastructure. The 2010 Haiti earthquake is an effective case study for the use of United States civil affairs forces in a large-scale humanitarian response.

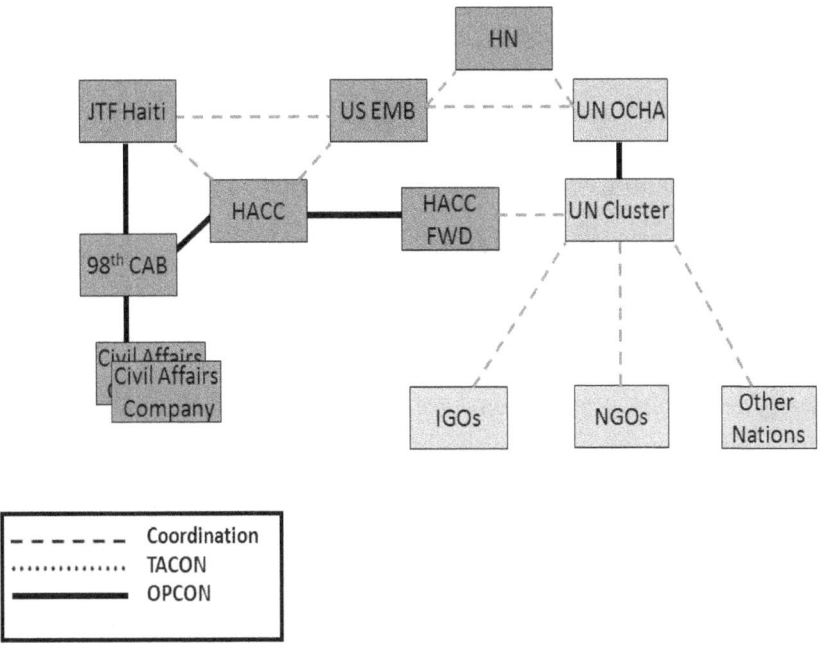

Figure 6.   Operations Unified Response Organization and Relationships for CA

Source. Patrick Blakenship, "Into Haiti," *Special Warfare Magazine* (September-October 2010), 27.

The scale of the disaster in Haiti precipitated SOCOM directing the 98th Civil Affairs Battalion to deploy immediately to Haiti. The initial elements from the battalion headquarters made up the Humanitarian Assistance Coordination Center (HACC). The HACC operated out of the United States embassy and served as the JTF's liaison element with the State Department and USAID. The figure above demonstrates the complicated relationships between the United States military, the United States Embassy, OCHA, and the IGOs and NGOS that comprised the cluster system. The main role the 98th Civil

Affairs Battalion initially filled was building relationships within the embassy and acting as the coordination cell between the Embassy and JTF-Haiti.[47]

Earlier analysis established the need to provide a coordination center or HACC to coordinate between United States joint forces, the United States interagency, civilian aid organizations, and the South Korean government and that FM 3-57 directs civil affairs to conducting that coordination task. The JTF in Haiti required the 98th Civil Affairs Battalion to provide a HACC to the US Embassy and a HACC forward to the United Nations cluster system.

United Nations OCHA established the cluster system as it arrived in Haiti. United States doctrine directs civil affairs to work as a coordination element with JIIM partners through CMOCs or HACCs. Elements from USAID, State, and the 98th CA Battalion would form a HACC forward to facilitate communication between the United Nations, JTF, and United States Embassy.[48] The HACC forward was the means the United States interagency used to share information with the United Nations and civilian aid organization. Additionally, the HACC forward served as the collection point for assistance requests from the cluster system to JTF-Haiti. The HACC forward would only accept support requests routed through United Nations OCHA and approved by the lead agency in the cluster system.[49] The HACC forward ensured that United States assistance was in line with international standards.

The civil affairs teams played a key role early in the Haiti humanitarian response by conducting civil reconnaissance. The 98th Civil Affairs battalion had two companies with additional elements task organized to them. The 98th pushed the company headquarters out to more remote locations to help keep JTF-Haiti informed of humanitarian issues and events happening outside of Port-au-Prince.[50] Civil affairs teams deployed rapidly and were able to begin conducting assessments early. Additionally, Haiti had security issues with gangs openly carrying weapons.[51] Civil affairs teams train to work in small elements in hostile areas. The civil affairs teams in Haiti were able to provide early assessments to JTF-Haiti despite security threats.

The immediate effort of the humanitarian response was to relieve human suffering and the need was greatest among the 1.5 million dislocated Haitian civilians.[52] A focus of the 98th CA Battalion was to identify dislocated civilians and locations for DC camps.[53] Civil affairs located, produced maps, and shared the information for DC camps on the All Partners Access Network (APAN) so civilian aid agencies could get access to the information.[54] The figure below illustrates a map of IDP camps the 98th Civil Affairs Battalion produced in a geospatial database and then shared with partner organizations on APAN. APAN is a dot org server that United States Pacific Command maintains to share disaster assistance information. JTF Haiti mandated use of APAN to ensure United States military information was available to its civilian partners. United States civil affairs ability to deploy rapidly, conduct civil reconnaissance, identify DC camps and share the information across the JIIM environment makes CA an integral part of a United States military response to disasters.

IDP CAMPS

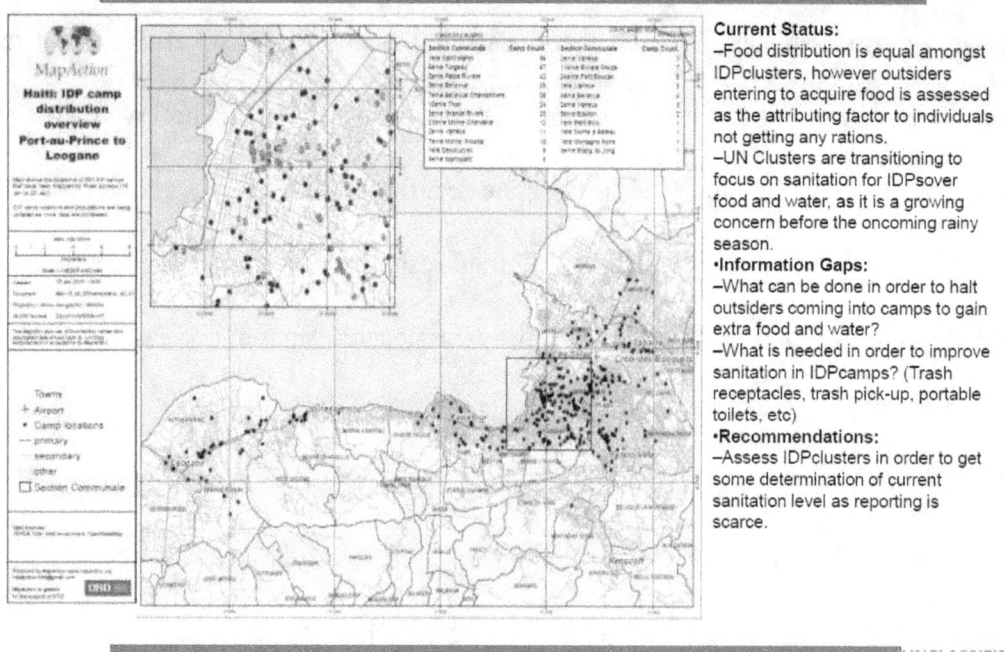

Current Status:
−Food distribution is equal amongst IDPclusters, however outsiders entering to acquire food is assessed as the attributing factor to individuals not getting any rations.
−UN Clusters are transitioning to focus on sanitation for IDPsover food and water, as it is a growing concern before the oncoming rainy season.
•**Information Gaps:**
−What can be done in order to halt outsiders coming into camps to gain extra food and water?
−What is needed in order to improve sanitation in IDPcamps? (Trash receptacles, trash pick-up, portable toilets, etc)
•**Recommendations:**
−Assess IDPclusters in order to get some determination of current sanitation level as reporting is scarce.

Figure 7.   IDP update from 98th CS Battalion brief by LTC Stevens

Source. Joseph Stevens, "98th CA BN (A) Brief on Operation Unified Response," (2010 Global Civil Affairs Conference at Fort Bragg, NC, February 2010), 13.

In addition to settling dislocated civilians, the 98th Civil Affairs Battalion assisted in coordinating and delivering food aid. The 98th Civil Affairs Battalion worked with the World Food Program, the logistics lead responsible for food delivery in the United Nations cluster system, to assist the delivery of food aid. JTF-Haiti made food aid delivery through the World Food Program its first priority.[55] Teams from the 98th were particularly effective in delivering aid to Haitians in more remote areas. Civil affairs teams located near the city of Hinche worked with NGOs and the local government to ensure they properly sent and processed their food aid requests through the United

Nations cluster system.[56] Coordinating efforts between the JTF, the local governments, and the United Nations cluster system ensured food aid went where needed in a manner consistent with international standards.

Civil affairs provided medical assistance to some Haitians as part of a larger effort to triage and treat the more than half million wounded Haitians. A civil affairs battalion is manned with a surgical doctor, a veterinarian, and Special Operations Combat Medics.[57] The surgeon and veterinarian are only at the battalion level, but the Operations Combat Medics are on every team. The most significant role civil affairs played in Haiti was their ability to find, triage, and transport patients to higher levels of care.[58] The photograph below shows a civil affairs medic transporting a patient from a remote area to Port-au-Prince for treatment. Civil affairs is uniquely suited to provide medical assistance in remote areas in the immediate aftermath of a disaster or humanitarian crisis.

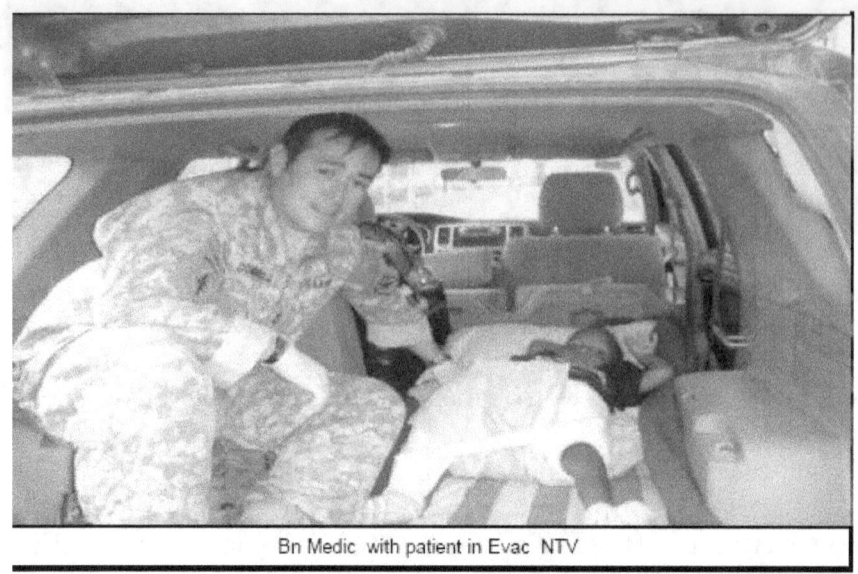

Bn Medic with patient in Evac NTV

Figure 8.   Civil Affairs medic treating pelvic fracture and preparing for evacuation to Port-au-Prince, Haiti

Source. Joseph Stevens, "98th CA BN (A) Brief on Operation Unified Response," (2010 Global Civil Affairs Conference at Fort Bragg, NC, February 2010), 18.

The 98th Civil Affairs Battalion (A) played an integral role in the United States military's response to the 2010 earthquake in Haiti. The first role the military played was as a coordination center between the interagency, intergovernmental organizations, and other civilian aid agencies. The 98th CA Battalion did this through the HACC, located at the United States Embassy, and through the HACC Froward, collocated with the United Nations cluster system. The civil affairs core task of Civil Information Management facilitated the 98ths coordination efforts. The 98th conducted CIM by conducting civil reconnaissance to complete early assessments, collating the information, developing products like IDP maps on a geospatial format, and then sharing the information on a non-government server such as APAN to ensure civilian partners would have access to the products. The coordination and information sharing facilitated the provision of temporary shelters, food aid, and medical assistance to displaced persons. The 2010 Haiti earthquake case study shows United States civil affairs provides a unique capability, supported by doctrine and training, to facilitate a United States military response to a large-scale humanitarian crisis.

The analysis in this paper demonstrates five main areas where United States civil affairs has a niche role in a response to the impending collapse of the North Korean Regime. Approximately 480,000 dislocated civilians are likely to emerge following the collapse of North Korea. Tasks in joint and service doctrine direct civil affairs to facilitate the identification of camps, assist the settlement of DCs, and ensure DC treatment meets internationally accepted standards. Most North Koreans and DCs in particular will require food, water, and health assistance. FHA is a CA core task and directs CA in the delivery of humanitarian assistance. Working with many governmental and civilian aid agencies is a complex environment. Doctrine provides a niche role for civil affairs to work as a coordination center and developing and disseminating civil information to ensure civilian aid agencies view the same problem as the JTF or United Nations OCHA. The 2010 Haiti earthquake demonstrated the historical use of civil affairs in a humanitarian crisis scenario similar to that expected in North Korea following a collapse of the North Korean Regime. United States civil affairs will use the core task of Nation Assistance to prepare for the pending North Korean humanitarian crisis.

---

[1]The Sphere Project, 243.

[2]Ibid., 256.

[3]Ibid., 114.

[4]Ibid., 257.

[5]Ibid.

[6]Ibid., 258.

[7]Ibid., 35.

[8]Justin McCury, "No End in Sight for North Korea's Malnutrition Crisis," *The Lance* 379, no. 18 (February 2012): 602.

[9]Ibid.

[10]The Sphere Project, 34.

[11]Leon Goe, "Community-based public health interventions in North Korea: One non-governmental organizations' experience with tuberculosis," *Journal of the Royal Institute of Public Health* (30 March 2004): 3.

[12]The Sphere Project, 59.

[13]United States Department of Defense, Joint Publication 3-29, *Foreign Humanitarian Assistance* (Washington, DC: Government Printing Office, 2011), ix.

[14]Walter Kalin, "Guiding Priciples on Internal Displacement," *Studies in Transnational Legal Policy* no. 38 (2008): 90.

[15]Woo-Sung Jung and Fengzhou Wang, "Gravity Model in the Korean Highway," Department of Physics, Boston University. 2 February 2010, 3.

[16]Ceasar Ducruet, "Coastal cities, port activities and logistic constraints in a socialist developing country: The case of North Korea," *Transport Reviews* 28 (2008): 1.

[17]Ibid., 29.

[18]Ibid., 30.

[19]Ibid., 13.

[20]United States Department of Defense, Joint Publication 3-05, *Special Operations* (Washington, DC: Government Printing Office, 2011), IV-1.

[21]Ibid.

[22]Ibid., 3-2.

[23]Ibid., 3-4.

[24]United States Department of the Army, FM 3-57, *Civil Affairs Operations,* 3-6.

[25]Ibid., 3-6.

[26]The Sphere Project, 212.

[27]Ibid., 3-6.

[28]Ibid.

[29]Ibid., 3-8.

[30]Ibid., 3-9.

[31]United Nations Office for the Coordination of Humanitarian Affairs, "How are disaster relief efforts organised? Cluster Approach," http://business.un.org/en/.../ 39c87a78-fec9-402e-a434-2c355f24e4f4.pdf (accessed 3 April 2012).

[32]Ibid.

[33]Ibid., 3-10.

[34]Ibid., 3-12.

[35]Ibid., 3-11.

[36]Ibid., 3-13.

[37]Ibid., 3-12.

[38]Ibid., 3-9.

[39]Ibid., 3-13.

[40]Ibid., 3-14.

[41]Ibid., 3-15.

[42]Ibid., 3-8.

[43]Blakenship, "Into Haiti," 25.

[44]Special Operations Command Public Affairs, "Civil Affairs makes a difference in Haiti following massive earthquake," *Tip of the Spear* (April 2010), 6.

[45]Schuller, "Haiti's Disaster after the Disaster: The IDP Camps and Cholera," 1

[46]Blakenship, "Into Haiti," 27.

[47]Special Operations Command Public Affairs, "Civil Affairs makes a difference in Haiti following massive earthquake," 6.

[48]Blakenship, "Into Haiti," 27.

[49]Ibid., 28.

[50]Joseph Stevens, "98th CA BN (A) Brief on Operation Unified Response" (2010 Global Civil Affairs Conference at Fort Bragg, NC, February 2010), 2.

[51]Ibid., 1.

[52]Schuller, "Haiti's Disaster after the Disaster: The IDP Camps and Cholera," 1.

[53]Special Operations Command Public Affairs, "Civil Affairs makes a difference in Haiti following massive earthquake," 7.

[54]Stevens, "98th CA BN (A) Brief on Operation Unified Response," 23.

[55]Ibid., 24.

[56] Special Operations Command Public Affairs, "Civil Affairs makes a difference in Haiti following massive earthquake," 7.

[57]United States Department of the Army, FM 3-57, *Civil Affairs Operations,* 2-11.

[58]Special Operations Command Public Affairs, "Civil Affairs makes a difference in Haiti following massive earthquake," 7.

CHAPTER 5

RECOMMENDATIONS AND CONCLUSIONS

An analysis of the projected scope of the disaster, civil affairs doctrine, and the case study of the 2010 Haiti earthquake shows a possible niche role for civil affairs in a humanitarian response when the North Korean regime collapses. Those tasks are assisting with settling dislocated civilians; humanitarian assistance such as food, water, and health care; coordination across JIIM actors; and civil information management to include civil reconnaissance. This study will make a few recommendations on how United States civil affairs forces can prepare for a post-collapse humanitarian crisis on the Korean peninsula. Those preparations will take the form of training United States civil affairs units, training other military forces, and making physical preparations for an eventual collapse.

Settlement of Dislocated Civilians

Civil affairs planners and civil affairs units need to conduct several tasks to prepare to assist with the settlement of dislocated civilians following the collapse of North Korea. Civil affairs needs to conduct planning, training, and physical preparations to ensure the United States military is prepared for the humanitarian crisis following the collapse of the North Korean regime.

Civil affairs planners need to ensure contingency plans consider the scope of the problem outlined in the analysis, consider international standards for the settlement of DCs, and lessons learned from Haiti on the settlement of dislocated civilians. By comparing the number of expected DCs, against the *Sphere Project Handbook* minimal

65

standards for DC camps civil affairs planners can determine the space requirements and the types and amount of units to secure the camps.

Civil affairs units need to consider the space requirements and begin training for the humanitarian response mission in a post-collapse Korea. The units need to begin with individual and collective training on the populace and resource control tasks in FM 3-57. The preparation for training should include terrain analysis to identify possible sites for DC camps following the collapse of the North Korean Regime. Unit training should include time to work with geospatial mapping tools to find terrain with the space and slope requirements to meet international standards for DC camps. That analysis would direct future reconnaissance efforts to save time when United States civil affairs units participate in exercises with their South Korean counterparts.

Civil affairs units need to become more involved in combined exercises with Korea to ensure their ability to work dislocated civilian issues with their South Korean counter parts. The United States conducts two bilateral training exercises with the Republic of Korea. The two exercises are Ulchi Focus Lens and Foal Eagle. Ulchi Focus Lens is primarily a command post exercise conducted in the August to September period.[1] Foal Eagle is a combined force exercise typically conducted at the beginning of the year.[2] Civil affairs units and their Korean counter parts can use the training events as a chance to check possible sites for camps from terrain analysis and confirm or deny that the space is suitable for dislocated civilians to settle. Civil affairs units must become more involved in Ulchi Focus Lens and Foal Eagle focused on a humanitarian response following the collapse of the North Korean regime.

Humanitarian Assistance

Civil affairs units should prepare to conduct foreign humanitarian assistance following the collapse of the North Korean regime. Civil affairs units take advantage of Joint Combined Exchange Training (JCETs) in Korea, use the JCETs to execute FHA programs in preparation of a humanitarian crisis, and work with IGOs and NGOs to identify commodities, primarily food, that South Korea and its allies need to secure.

Civil affairs units must become more active in Special Operations Command Pacific's Joint Combined Exchange Training events in Korea.[3] These events often run for a month conducted for up to a 45 day period with host nation special operations forces. The purpose of the exercise is for United States special operations forces to work on their mission essential tasks in a regional environment. The exercises have the additional benefit of developing partnerships and interoperability with the host nation force. The regular training venues to exercise United States civil affairs humanitarian response capabilities on the terrain where the event could occur would be invaluable. Additionally, the opportunity to conduct the training with host nation forces to develop interoperability and reduce friction before a crisis event occurs.

United States civil affairs can conduct humanitarian civic action programs as a part of their JCET to prepare future DC camps. The HCA programs could pay for humanitarian projects that were incidental to United States military training events and would help prepare South Korea to manage a humanitarian crisis in a post-collapse Korea. HCA programs would benefit the United States and the Korean public at the time of a humanitarian crisis.

Civil affairs planners should try to identify IGOs or NGOs that work on the Korean peninsula that could be future partners. IGOs like the World Food Program and the Red Cross have experience providing aid to North Korea.[4] IGOs and NGOs can provide and understanding of the issues concerning food shortages and health. Additionally, IGOs and NGOs could help identify food storage facilities. Identifying food storage facilities to ensure South Korea and its allies will be able to secure the facilities. Current food facilities will reduce the amount of aid humanitarian actors will have to ship into country.

<u>Civil Information Management and JIIM Coordination</u>

Civil affairs planners need to accomplish two major tasks to ensure integration of all JIIM partners. Civil affairs planners need to compile all the civil information CA units gather and ensure the widest dissemination. One of the exercises in Korea should include United Nations OCHA as well as American and South Korean forces. The first time South Korea, the United States, and OCHA rehearse coordination and communication should not be during a crisis. Civil affairs planners can prepare for an impending humanitarian crisis following the collapse of the North Korean regime by sharing information as widely as possible and ensuring humanitarian actors at the highest levels have a mutual understanding of the problem and each other's capabilities.

Civil affairs planners need to share the civil data garnered from units conducting civil reconnaissance in South Korea and data gathered from IGOs and NGOs that work in South Korea. Civil Affairs planners need to share their layered geospatial information and the background data on a sever open to the largest public. Civil Affairs planners should take a lesson learned from JTF Haiti and use APAN or a similar site available to the public to post all civil data. If government agencies, IGOs, and NGOs have the same information available to them before and during a crisis, it will be easier for South Korea and OCHA to organize humanitarian efforts.

Civil affairs planners should begin contact with OCHA to plan and coordinate early efforts as a response to a possible humanitarian crisis on the Korean peninsula. OCHA will be the lead organization for the international response to a crisis on the Korean peninsula. United States civil affairs should keep track of all OCHA conferences on North Korea. Building relationships with United Nations partners before the crisis will facilitate the international response when the international response does happen.

One of the United States and South Korean combined exercises should include OCHA and focus on a post-collapse humanitarian response. The exercise could be at least a staff exercise to ensure the leadership of the different organizations can synchronize planning and execution, but the two countries would gain more if brigade-sized units were a part of the exercise. Additionally, the exercises could build the capacity of individual South Korean units to work in a humanitarian scenario and the interoperability of United States and South Korean troops.

Civil affairs planners need to prepare for the collapse of the North Korean regime and the humanitarian crisis that will follow. Civil affairs planners need to work on sites for dislocated civilians, plans to secure commodities, building the civil database for humanitarian response, training for a humanitarian response with partners, and building relationships with joint, interagency. intergovernmental, and multinational partners. Any success in post-collapse humanitarian response will stem from early planning and good relationships among humanitarian actors involved in a future humanitarian operation.

Suggestions for Further Research

This study did not consider China's reaction to a collapse, or how China's reaction could affect the humanitarian response. Japan, China, and Russia all have strategic interests in North Korea. China has the most to lose were North Korea to fall and the entire peninsula unified under the Republic of Korea. A future study could try to answer what it would mean to humanitarian response efforts following a collapse of the North Korean regime were China to become directly involved.

David Coghlan in his paper, "Prospects from Korean Unification," states that China could set up a buffer zone South of the Yalu river for two purposes.[5] One is to ensure Chinese interests in the outcomes in a possible unification following the regime's collapse. The second is to manage North Korean migration to China. The clash of geo-political interests between the United States and China could affect humanitarian operations and limit American involvement. A research paper determining the effects China's involvement in a post-collapse North Korea would have on humanitarian operations and the United States involvement in the operation is a topic the deserves additional study..

Additionally, this study did not consider the psychological impacts North Korean propaganda has caused the North Korean people. How will life in the "Hermit Kingdom" affect the conduct of humanitarian assistance missions? The philosophy of Juche, constant propaganda, and the regime's absolute control over the population has caused psychological damage to the North Korean people.[6] It is likely that the effects of a closed society and the philosophy of Juche could hamper humanitarian efforts.

70

Juche means self-reliance and dictates that North Koreans are an independent people that do not need outside assistance. Juche combined with constant propaganda by the Kim regime that paints South Korea as a puppet of an evil imperialist American government. It is likely that Juche and decades of propaganda will affect humanitarian operations and could limit direct American involvement with North Koreans. The topic of the psychological effects of living in the DPRK and effects on humanitarian operations and American involvement in a humanitarian response is a topic that deserves further study.

---

[1] http://www.globalsecurity.org/military/ops/ulchi-focus-lens.htm (accessed 1 May 2012).

[2] http://www.globalsecurity.org/military/ops/foal-eagle.htm (accessed 3 May 2012).

[3] http://www.gao.gov/products/NSIAD-99-173 (accessed 3 May 2012).

[4] McCury, "No End in Sight for North Korea's Malnutrition Crisis," 602.

[5] David Coghlan, (Prospects from Korean Unification) Carlisle: Strategic Studies Institute, April 2008), 9.

[6] O, "The Integration of North Korean Defectors in South Korea: Problems and Prospects," 155.

BIBLIOGRAPHY

Books

Coghlan, David. "Prospects from Korean Unification." Carlisle Papers, Strategic Studies Institute, 2008.

Eberstadt, Nicholas. *Korea's Future and the Great Powers.* United States: The National Bureau of Asian Research, 2001.

Ford, Glyn. *North Korea on the Brink:Struggle for Survival*. London: Pluto Press, 2008.

Key-Young, Son. *South Korean Engagement Policies and the Sunshine Policy*. New York: Routledge, 2006.

Oh, Dan, and Ralph C Hassig. *North Korea Through the Looking Glass.* Washington DC: Brookings Institution Press, 2000.

Phillip W Yun and Gi-Wook Shin. *North Korea: 2005 and Beyond.* Stanford: Brookings Institution Press, 2005.

Savada, Andrea Matles. *North Korea: A Country Study*. Washington, DC: Library of Congress. 1999.

Scobell, Andrew. *Projecting Pyang Yang: The Future of North Korea's Kim Jong Il Regime*. Carlisle: Strategic Studies Institute, 2008.

Wolf Jr, Charles, and Kamil Akramov. *North Korean Paradoxes:Circumstances, Costs, and Consequences of Korean Unification.* Study, National Defense Research Institute, Santa Monica: Rand, 2005.

Journals

Blakenship, Patrick. "Into Haiti." *Special Warfare Magazine* (September-October 2010).

Ducruet, Ceasar. "Coastal cities, port activities and logistic constraints in a socialist developing country: The case of North Korea." *Transport Reviews* 28 (2008): 1-25.

Gill, Bates. *China's North Korea Policy.* Special Report 283. Washington DC: United States Institue of Peace, 2011.

Goe, Leon. "Community-based public health interventions in North Korea: One non-governmental organizations' experience with tuberculosis." *Journal of the Royal Institute of Public Health*. 30 March 2004.

Joo, Seung-Ho. "North Korea Under Kim Jong-un: The Beginning of the End of a Peculiar Dynasty." *Pacific Focus* 27, no. 1 (April 2012): 1–9.

Kalin, Walter. "Guiding Priciples on Internal Displacement." *Studies in Transnational Legal Policy*. no 38, 2008.

Kelly, Robert. "The German-Korean Unification Parallel." *The Korean Journal of Defense Analysis* 23, no. 4 (December 2011): 457-472.

Lee, Grace. "The Political Philosophy of Juche." *Stanford Journal of East Asian Affiars* 3, no. 1 (January 2007): 105-112.

McCury, Justin. "No End in Sight for North Korea's Malnutrition Crisis." *The Lancet*. 379, no. 18 (February 2012).

O, Tara. "The Integration of North Korean Defectors in South Korea: Problems and Prospects." *International Journal of Korean Studies* 15, no. 2 (June 2011): 151-169

Schuller, Mark. "Haiti's Disaster after the Disaster: The IDP Camps and Cholera." *The Journal of Humanitarian Assistance* (December 2011).

Snyder, Scott A. "Instability in North Korea and Its Impact on US China Relations." *Council of Foreign Relations* (2009): 11-24.

Special Operations Command Public Affairs. "Civil Affairs makes a difference in Haiti following massive earthquake." *Tip of the Spear*. April 2010.

Stares, Paul B. and Joel S. Wit. "Preparing for Sudden Change in North Korea," *Council on Foreign Relations* Special Report No. 42 (January 2009).

Government Documents

Government Accounting Office. *United States Bilateral Food Assistance to North Korea Had Mixed Results.* Report to the Chairman and Ranking Minority Member, Committee on Internaional Relations, Washington, DC: Government Accounting Office, 2000.

Margesson, Rhoda. *Haiti Earthquake: Crisis and Response.* Washington, DC: Congressional Research Service, 2010.

United States Department of the Air Force. AFDD 2-3, *Military Operations Other Than War.* Washington, DC: Government Printing Office, 2003.

———. AFDD 2-4.2, *Health Services.* Washington, DC: Government Printing Office, 2003.

United States Department of the Army. FM 1-02, *Operational Terms and Graphis*. Washington, DC: Government Printing Office, 2011.

————. FM 3-05, *Special Operations*. Washington, DC: Government Printing Office, 2004.

————. FM 3-05.401, *Civil Affairs Tactics Techniques and Procedures*. Washington, DC: Government Printing Office, 2007.

————. FM 3-57, *Civil Affairs Operations*. Washington, DC: Government Printing Office, 2011.

United States Department of Defense. Joint Publication 3-05, *Special Operations*. Washington, DC: Government Printing Office, 2011.

————. Joint Publication 3-29, *Foreign Humanitarian Assistance*. Washington, DC: Government Printing Office, 2011.

————. Joint Publication 3-57, *Civil Military Operations*. Washington, DC: Government Printing Office, 2011.

United States Marine Corps. MCWP 3-33.1, Marine *Air-Ground Task Force Civil-Military Operations*. Washington, DC: Government Printing Office, 2004.

Other Sources

Choi, Seung Mo. Economic Impacts of Reunifications in Germany and Korea. Washington State School of Economics, December 2011.

Kim, Ki Hwan. "ROK Army Manpower Force Structure." Naval Postgraduate School, Monterey, 2006.

Lee, Hyun. "An Analysis of the Size and Structure of the Army of Reunified Korea." Monterey: Naval Postgraduate School, 2010.

Maxwell, David S. "Irregular Warfare on the Korean Peninsula: Thoughts on Irregular Threats for North Korea Post-Conflict and Post-Collapse: Understanding Them to Counter Them." *Small Wars Journal* (November 2010). http://smallwars journal.com/jrnl/art/irregular-warfare-on-the-korean-peninsula. (accessed 13 October 2011).

Pollack, Jonathon, and Chung Min Lee. *Preparing for Korean Unification*. Santa Monica: RAND, 1999.

Sang-Hun, Choe. "Economic Measures by North Korea Prompt New Hardships and Unrest." *The New York Times*, 4 February 2010.

The Sphere Project. *Humanitarian Charter and Minimum Standards in Humanitarian Response*. 3rd ed. United Kingdom: Practical Action Publishing, 2011.

Stevens, Joseph. "98th CA BN (A) Brief on Operation Unified Response." 2010 Global Civil Affairs Conference, Fort Bragg, NC. February 2010.

United Nations Office for the Coordination of Humanitarian Affairs. "How are disaster relief efforts organised? Cluster Approach." http://business.un.org/en/.../ 39c87a78-fec9-402e-a434-2c355f24e4f4.pdf (accessed 3 April 2012).

Woo-Sung Jung and Fengzhou Wang. "Gravity Model in the Korean Highway." Department of Physics, Boston University, 2 February 2010.